Mrs. Sigourney

Published on the
Henry L. Johnson Memorial Fund

Lydia H. Sigourney

From a Painting by John Trumbull, 1838. By Permission
of The Wadsworth Atheneum.

Mrs. Sigourney

The Sweet Singer of Hartford

BY

GORDON S. HAIGHT

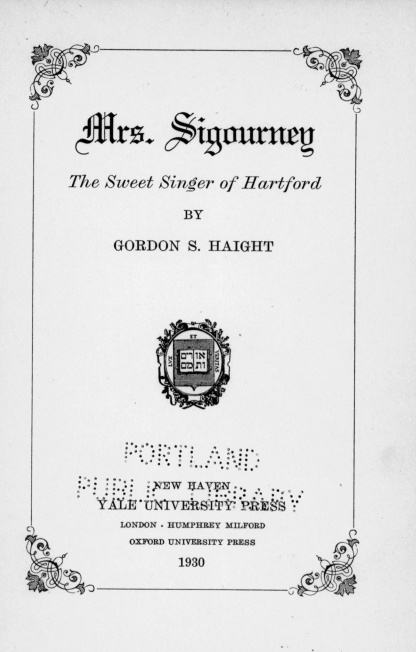

NEW HAVEN
YALE UNIVERSITY PRESS
LONDON · HUMPHREY MILFORD
OXFORD UNIVERSITY PRESS
1930

As a Slight
ACKNOWLEDGMENT
Of Ten Years of Most Devoted Friendship
THIS BOOK
Is Affectionately Dedicated To
CHARLES WHITE WHITTLESEY

PREFACE

*T*HE modern biographer is sometimes accused of disinterring the bones of his ancestors solely for the amusement of a profane generation. Nothing could have been farther from my thoughts in undertaking this study of Mrs. Sigourney. I hoped to find among her poems some few pieces that would establish her right to the reputation she enjoyed for half a century as America's leading poetess. But before reading many of the forty-odd volumes through which the search ultimately led me, I was forced to agree that posterity had judged fairly in denying her claim. I began then to wonder how she had achieved and maintained such popularity. Pursuit of this question revealed Mrs. Sigourney's wide acquaintance with famous people both at home and abroad during a lifetime that stretched from Washington's second term as President beyond the death of Lincoln.

Most of the present work is based upon her voluminous correspondence now in the keeping of the Connecticut Historical Society, for the use of which I would here express my appreciation. For permission to use other manuscript material I am indebted to the New York Public Library, the New York Historical Society, the Boston Public Library, the Historical Society of Pennsylvania, the Texas State Library, the Berkshire Athenaeum and

Museum, and Trinity College. The fine Sigourney collection in the Watkinson Library of Hartford has proved very helpful. To the Yale University Library I am most grateful both for access to the Aldis collection, for the use of letters, and for the unfailing assistance of the Library staff.

Among the many individuals to whom I am obliged for letters and other assistance I would mention Mr. and Mrs. C. Morgan Aldrich, Mr. George Dudley Seymour, Dr. William M. Bradshaw, Mrs. Elford Trowbridge, Mr. James Hillhouse, Mrs. Russell G. Andrews, Mr. Edward C. Roberts, Mrs. Francis W. Tully, Mr. Jerome F. Milkman, Mrs. Joseph R. Noyes, Miss Sarah Carrington, Mr. Garland Greever, Dr. George F. Smythe, Miss Katharine C. Rockwood, Mr. Ernest W. Clement, Mr. Albert C. Bates, Mr. Frank B. Gay, Mr. George Van Santvoord, and Mr. John McChesney; and I cannot close the list without particular and affectionate reference to Mrs. Thomas B. Chapman, who first introduced me to Mrs. Sigourney, and Professor Stanley T. Williams, who encouraged me to cultivate the acquaintance.

G. S. H.

The Hotchkiss School
Lakeville, Connecticut
May, 1930

CONTENTS

LIST OF ILLUSTRATIONS

CHAPTER ONE

"THE BROKEN FLOW'RET"

JN 1805 the southern part of Norwich was a cluster of neat little houses perched on the steep bank of the Thames. Streets rose above streets so precipitously that the foundations of one line sometimes overtopped the roofs of another, and below you saw the masts of river boats peering over the warehouses, where they were discharging their cargoes of farm implements and molasses. But the northern part of the town a mile beyond was quite different in aspect, with rolling meadows, and amply spaced houses overshadowed by lofty elms. Here, separated from the road by a tidy white fence, stood the simple colonial dwelling of the Widow Lathrop, with sweetbriar climbing above the second story to the roof. After passing between the spruce trees at the gate, you saw the vegetable gardens stretching far down to the right. Around behind the house were the orchards; and closer by, a nursery of medicinal herbs—sage, hoarhound, cumfrey, tansy, rue, and wormwood—that the late Dr. Lathrop had planted to supply his apothecary shop. In the flower garden to the left of the house the phlox and peonies left room for such humbler blossoms as mourning bride and fumitory.

It was one of those mild September evenings that foretell the end of summer, and lure everyone out of doors. But the only person in sight was the gardener, who was filling an old-fashioned watering can at the well. All the other members of the household were gathered within the house, where Madam Lathrop lay dying. She was eighty-eight years old. During the long decay of senility, her chief solace had come from the gardener's daughter, Lydia Huntley, a slender child, barely fourteen, who now knelt at her bedside. Lydia's attentions had by no means been confined to bowls of gruel and pillow-smoothing. She ministered to the mind, calming the old lady's restless inquiries about household affairs or reciting her will "with its full list of legacies, donations, and charitable bequests."[1] Sometimes within the curtains of the bed, her smooth, pale cheek joined to Madam Lathrop's, she would sing the old-fashioned melodies that lulled her to sleep. But last night the invalid had grown delirious and cried out wildly a snatch of one of the songs, and today she had not recognized those about her.

Dr. Daniel Lathrop, after graduating from Yale in 1733, had studied medicine in London. With a stock of drugs brought with him on his return, he set up in the apothecary business in a shop opposite his house, which enjoyed great prosperity as the only one on the post road between New York and Boston. One of his apprentices was Benedict Arnold, whose subsequent treachery brought forth from those who had known him in youth apocryphal anecdotes of maltreated cats, desolated birds' nests, misused schoolbooks, and dare-devil stunts performed on a moving mill wheel.[2] But he had gone into the drug trade for himself several years before Dr. Lathrop hired Ezekiel Huntley to do the chores. Zeke was a slow, rawboned Connecticut youth; but he did his work so faithfully that after the Doctor's death in 1782 Madam Lathrop continued to employ him as gardener.

He joined the first regiment formed after the battle of Lexington, and saw honorable service in the Revolution.[3] Then, coming back to Norwich, he married Lydia Howard, a gentle creature who died of tuberculosis before her first wedding anniversary. Three years later, at the age of forty, he took as his second wife, Zerviah Wentworth,[4] a pretty girl of twenty-three. On September 1, 1791, their only child was born, and within a week, following a not uncommon practice,[5] christened Lydia Howard Huntley, after ''the early smitten consort.''

Lydia's recollections of her father reveal more of herself than of him. The ardor of her attachment might offer psychiatrists an interesting study. Part of her work in the household was to provide his clothes; before she was twelve she made his shirts, his stockings (with a special ribbing that better displayed ''the symmetry of his well-shaped limbs''),[6] and even a suit of homespun. Mr. Huntley never praised the eager little seamstress.

I cannot recollect [she wrote] that he ever thanked me. I would not have had him; it would have troubled me. The holy intonation of his voice when he said *"My child,"* was enough. The sweetest tears swelled under my eyelids when I thought of him. Methinks the love of a daughter for a father is distinct and different from all other loves.[7]

But to a dispassionate observer this idol was simply Madam Lathrop's hired man, blunt, honest, severely conventional, and quite preoccupied with the practical affairs of life.

Lydia inherited some of these qualities from her

father; but it was to her mother that she owed her sympathy and quickness. Though Mrs. Huntley had received little education, she read everything she could lay hands on. She was the person who borrowed *The Mysteries of Udolpho,* from which Lydia, hidden in a trunk in the attic, derived such delicious surreptitious thrills. She was the one who encouraged the child of eight to write a novel "in the epistolary style, and a part of the scene laid in Italy."[8] It was with her guidance, too, that ten-year-old Lydia selected for her first large water color Maria, "the crazy girl described by the sentimental Yorick," with Sterne "at a distance, taking note of her with an eye-glass. . . ."[9] Needless to say, there went with all this a good-natured, but thorough, instruction in all the details of housekeeping.

Sometimes Madam Lathrop would invite the little child from across the hall into her parlor, where the light shining from the two old-fashioned candlesticks was reflected in the ebony-framed mirror and the dark, polished wainscot. Seated in her cushioned armchair by a brightly blazing fire, the old lady would take her spectacles from between the leaves of Young's *Night Thoughts,* which lay with the Bible on a small, round table at her side, and hand the book to Lydia, who would read in a clear voice from "The Consolation," while Madam Lathrop, resting her brow on her hand, indulged in mournful reverie. She seemed to see her mother, "again smitten by an unseen hand, and covered suddenly with the paleness of the tomb"; once more the last words of her father "faltered on her ear, as she wiped the dews from his temples."[10] Then she fancied her husband sitting beside her; and finally, prattling about her chair, their three children, who had all died within a week of some infectious disease.

And Lydia's tears flowed in sympathy as she heard again the melancholy account of this tragedy.

Hours like these fostered in the girl the sentimentality that was to be her principal resource in later years. "The cream of all my happiness," she said of her childhood, "was a loving intercourse with venerable age."[11] At the sight of a very aged person the sentimentalists of the nineteenth century suffered nearly the same shiver of painful delight that the contemplation of the young consumptive caused them. Given some composure of countenance and enough wavy white hair, the most irascible old fellow becomes "that blessed" or "that sainted" old man. You have "parents, venerable in age, (—words that I can scarcely write without a tear)," says Lydia years later, in complimenting a friend on his happy family.[12] A spinster of fifty-three who exchanged letters with her on the subject, confesses even more.

Walking the streets, and in the most exuberent spirits, talking with a companion, if a trembling, white-haired aged man passes before me, I feel the tears gushing hot, and rolling down to quench the smile upon my lips, before I am aware of the change in my emotions. But it is not mourning nor sorrow that does this. I can only call it melting.[13]

And "melting" is an unmistakable mark of the sentimentalist.

Madam Lathrop's last illness gave Lydia opportunities for the exercise of "melting," which, up to that time, literature, measured by its power to draw tears, alone had supplied. Such bits as Gessner's *Death of Abel* and Hervey's *Meditations among the Tombs* could not compare with real meditations at the deathbed of a venerable friend. The end came.

She would fain have impressed one more kiss upon my brow, but her lips were powerless. I saw not when the last change passed, though I knelt beside her, my face buried in her pillow. I only remember that they said, *"She is gone!"* and that they carried me from the room.

The funeral was to me like a great, terrific dream. . . . I was conscious of a great crowd, but saw nothing. I heard the voice of solemn prayer, but followed not its words. The long procession moved onward to the church. I was lifted to the carriage and taken out, and set in the right place among the mourners, by whose hands I knew not.[14]

It is safe to say that at the funeral attention was fairly divided between the late Madam Lathrop and her faithful young friend. Such a spectacle of bereavement is not often seen. Acquaintances who stopped to inquire after the poor sparrow alone upon the housetop, as one clergyman called her, found the "suffocating pain with which Grief is wont to seize its victims by the throat" oppressing her whenever she tried to speak.[15] But the sentimentalist loves above all to share the secret sorrows, and Lydia saw to it that the fearful spasms that racked her were not concealed too carefully from her parents. Rather alarmed at her extraordinary symptoms, they called in Dr. Philemon Tracy, who with great wisdom prescribed a change of scene, or in her own words, that she "should be encased in soft, red flannel, and take a short journey to visit the relatives of my loved, lamented friend," the Wadsworths of Hartford.[16]

Old Mrs. Jeremiah Wadsworth lived in the great house on Main Street, where, during her husband's life, she had entertained Washington, Lafayette, and the other French generals, come to consult him as commissary of the French troops. Lydia had often heard of the Wadsworths from her late friend, but whatever awe she felt as she crossed the threshold was easily hidden in the flood of tears that "kept gushing out so forcibly" that she was ashamed to take her seat at the tea table.[17] Such palpable grief quite naturally enlisted all the sympathy of Mrs. Wadsworth and the two old spinster sisters-in-law who lived with her, and when they said good night there was much tenderness on both sides. Lying in bed, Lydia stroked the smooth, fine sheets as she listened to the church clocks striking nine, and reviewed carefully the scenes of the day. She recalled that Madam Lathrop had once said, "I wish I might have taken you to Hartford. Then you would have been received as my child." "My heart said to her: 'See, I have been so received.' "[18] And she went to sleep, confident and happy.

Behind the great house was one built by Colonel Wadsworth for his son Daniel, whose wife was a daughter of the second Governor Trumbull. In 1783 Colonel Wadsworth had gone to France to present his commissariat claims to the French Government, taking Daniel, then twelve years old, with him. The money he received was invested in manufactured goods of which the war had deprived the colonies for several years, and he sold them on his return at a handsome profit. His death in 1804 left Daniel a wealthy man, free to collect pictures and pose as the *arbiter elegantiae* and Maecenas of Hartford.

When Mrs. Wadsworth brought Lydia to call, the quick sparkle of delight in the child's eyes as she gazed in rapture at his books and paintings made a profound impression on Daniel. He knew her history, but had not expected to find such unusual grasp of language in the country girl of humble origin and little schooling. Of course she may borrow the Milton! There is no better

style for young writers to study. He had heard she wrote
verses. Perhaps she would show him some of them.

Miss Eunice Wadsworth gave Lydia a volume of Hannah More's *Sacred Dramas . . . to Which Are Added
Reflections of King Hezekiah, etc.*[19] And back in Norwich
two weeks later the child read again and again that monarch's query,

> Have I consider'd what it is to die?
> In native dust with kindred worms to lie?

and confided to her journal a hundred variations on the
death of Madam Lathrop. In the one called *Gratitude:
Lines written on planting slips of geranium and con-
stancy near the grave of a venerable friend* she pictures
herself bereft:

> And sick'ning on her lowly tomb
> The broken flow'ret lay.[20]

When the old house was sold, the Huntleys moved to a
small cottage where they could live most simply. But the
life of village housewife could never content the ambitious young lady who wanted to help support her parents, and whose help, moreover, was needed. Teaching was
the only career open to women at the time, and however
her quick mind and wide reading had fitted Lydia to give
instruction in the more substantial subjects, she was
quite unable to teach the superficial accomplishments
principally in demand. After an unsuccessful attempt to
start a school for girls in her own house, she went with a
friend, Nancy Maria Hyde, to Hartford to learn painting, embroidery, and filigree work, the "ornamental
branches" usually taught to young ladies. The Lydia

who called on the Wadsworths this time was not the sentimentalist, reveling in elaborate grief for her ancient
friend, but the twenty-year-old daughter of Aunt Lathrop's gardener, determined to raise herself to a position
of independence.

Miss Hyde and Miss Huntley opened their school at
Norwich in 1811[21] with tuition at the customary rate of
three dollars a quarter.[22] From the start Lydia was the
decisive half of the faculty. It was she who decreed that
each day should commence with extemporary prayer,[23] in
which she soon displayed impressive eloquence. It was
she who maintained the careful discipline, where Nancy's
sway proved too gentle. And when the school ended in
the winter of the second year, she had learned how to
teach, and had the satisfaction of having contributed to
the support of her parents.

In the spring of 1814 she was invited to visit the Wadsworths during the election festivities. Teaching and extemporary prayer had developed assurance, and the
pretty face and graceful wit proved wonderfully stimu-
lating to the old ladies on Main Street. Urged on by them,
Daniel Wadsworth resolved to see her established in the
world. Some touch of vanity may have prompted the idea
of fostering young genius, but his efforts were none the
less sincere.

His first step was to "gather a school" from among the
daughters of his friends. Fifteen girls from the first fami-
lies of Hartford were assembled in August, 1814, to
"pursue not solely the culture of the intellect, but the
education of the heart and life." Mrs. Willard, who had
opened her boarding school in Middlebury only six
months before, taught at first "the light, superficial
studies which were then considered suitable for girls"[24]

and introduced the higher subjects gradually. But Lydia
Huntley, backed by Mr. Wadsworth, excluded entirely
the "ornamental branches" so as not to divert attention
from the more solid subjects. The curriculum was still
comprehensive. Reading, Orthography with Definition,
Penmanship, Arithmetic, Rhetoric and Grammar, were
daily tasks, while "Ancient and Modern Geography, with
Natural and Moral Philosophy, were sources of mutual
enjoyment."[25] History was read aloud four afternoons a
week with special emphasis on Chronology. "When an
unemployed interval of only a few minutes occurred, I
was accustomed to ask them for a date," Lydia wrote,
"and, looking up with a bright smile, they would answer." The skill of the young pupils may be gauged by
some of the questions: "In what year of the world did
the ark rest upon Mount Ararat? Who was called, 1921
years before the Christian era, to go forth alone from his
people and his father's house? Who was Queen of As-
syria, and who the Judge of Israel, when Troy was de-
stroyed, 1184 years before Christ?"[26] Such questions,
glibly answered, must have pleased the parents and
friends, who assembled once a year to hear the general
examination that formed so important a feature of all
schools of the time.

If Lydia had continued teaching it seems likely that
her name would rank nearly as high as Emma Willard's
in the history of education for women. Both taught at
first with much the same methods. Both of them laid all
possible emphasis on the moral implication of the facts
learned, going even to the extent of rewriting history to
make the lives of Roman emperors illustrate virtues and
vices for children to read. But the result was undeniably
good; and what rigidity there may have been was sof-

tened by Miss Huntley's gentle methods. When the anniversary of the founding of the school came in 1815, the enthusiastic pupils planned a picnic in a neighboring grove; similar reunions held almost without omission for forty-five years after the school was discontinued[27] are the best testimony of Lydia's success as a teacher. In 1833, on the nineteenth anniversary, "anxious to testify to her their love, and gratitude," her former pupils presented her with a gold watch. "To her who so well feels the value of time [their note read], may this little monitor while it speaks of the present, recall 'by gone days,' which she has rendered to us so sweet in remembrance."[28]

Of greater significance was Mr. Wadsworth's second step in bringing before the public her first volume of poems. Asked ostensibly to judge of the suitability of some of them as reading exercises for the school, Mr. Wadsworth quickly saw the possibility of making them a source of income for his deserving young *protégée*. He gallantly undertook to make all the arrangements, and from Montevideo, his romantic country seat on Talcott Mountain, he offered some suggestions on the art of writing.

I send by Mrs. Irving the journal, and also the little poems which I am extremely glad you think of continuing. I am satisfied that it is not well for you to cramp yourself, by endeavoring to lower your stile to the capacity of children. Go on when ever you feel the inspiration, with as much glow & brilliancy as is consistent with perspicuity & freedom from affectation. *Do your best,* (as Doc[r] Johnson did in conversation) but do not hurry yourself.

I think this little work when completed will be an interesting, & creditable *second* volume—after you have become known by a *first*. Have no fears, I will take the responsibility of what is

done *at first* entirely on my-self, & I have no doubt but the result will be to you both profitable & honorable. Time is however
necessary in arranging a thousand things which relate to literary publications—Give my best love to Mama—tell her I took
no cold I am very well—Your friend, D. W.[29]

In the months that followed Mr. Wadsworth read all
the proof, changed words here and there, and wrote the
introduction, which he submitted to her at Norwich,
where she was spending the vacation with her parents.

After writing two or three little things by way of Preface—
your friends here all agree that the one [?] following, the most
simple, & short, of the whole, will be proper & all that is requisite.—Nothing would be necessary but for the purpose of let-
ting the Public know, that the Author has not had the advan-
tages of Affluence, & *a life of education,* among those, whose
literary taste, knowledge of the world, & elegant accomplishments, might render her acquirements only a matter of course.
—This simple statement of facts, will I think, without the appearance of asking forbearance, soften criticism. It is but
justice to yourself, that the Public should have some sense of
how entirely all you possess of literature has been from your
own exertions.—
    "A few of the Productions now bro^t before the Public were
"intended for the use of a School!—but the greater part arose
"from the impulse of the moment, at intervals of relaxation
"from such domestic employments, as the circumstances of the
"writer, and her Parents, rendered indispensible. Most of them
"were written when she was very young, & with the exception
"of two or three short pieces, the whole, before she had at-
"tained the age of twenty three years."
    If you do not approve this, let me know.

The letter closes with a message to the Huntleys that
shows very clearly Mr. Wadsworth's interest in his young
friend:

Give my best regards to your Father & Mother, & tell them
that I hope they will not make one objection to your complet-
ing your four quarters in the school here, as it is very essen-
tial now that you should establish a reputation which will in
future command a handsome independance.—If the children
under your care improve as I think they will, the credit it will
give you will be of lasting importance.[30]

Moral Pieces appeared early in 1815, the first of more
than fifty volumes published in a half century. It was
well named. Nothing she wrote could escape from her pen
without a moral. The simple formulas she established in
these poems remained practically unchanged throughout
her life. The first, the Historical Formula, includes such
political events as *The Conflagration at Washington* and
The Hartford Convention (then in session), as well as
little schoolroom lectures like *The Equanimity of Zeno,
Reply of the Philosopher Anaxarchus,* and *Paraphrase of
Cleopatra's Advice to Mark Anthony When Angling.*
The Religious Formula is represented by *The Distribution of Bibles at Malta, The Giving of the Bible to the
Esquimaux, The Departure of Mrs. Nott with the Missionaries for India,* and *The Destruction of the Inquisi-
tion at Goa,* all unquestionably moral. But her real forte
lay in poems on Death (with a capital D) ; and this formula, derived from the school of *Night Thoughts,* she
used almost without variation for fifty years, and with
such impartiality that a certain wag is said to have expressed a fear that she might survive to make him the
subject of an elegy. In this volume, however, her muse is
confined to *The Death of a Venerable Friend,* which appears in a dozen guises, with the faithful young author
always discernible not far from the pillow or the grave.

Advance subscriptions amounting to nearly a thousand

copies at a dollar each (a tribute to Daniel Wadsworth's wide acquaintance), there was little need for the lately founded *North American Review's* statement that Miss Huntley was "a most deserving and interesting young woman" who had "emancipated herself from the humblest penury, and still found leisure at a very early age, to compose this volume."[31] Readers must have enjoyed, however, the assurance that "the description of the deluge,

> And slowly as its axle turn'd
> The wat'ry planet moved and mourn'd"

was one of several in the poem *On the Dove's Leaving the Ark* "that partake of the sublime." And the proceeds must have seemed great indeed to the schoolmistress who had taught her pupils in Norwich for the sum of twelve dollars a year. As one of her gushing admirers described it, "the dutiful daughter, with overwhelming joy, laid the first fruits of her genius at the feet of her aged and straitened parents."

They, of course, made no objection to her continuing the school. To Mr. Huntley her success was highly gratifying; and her mother, more ambitious, looked to Hartford as a likely place for Lydia—now nearly twenty-five—to find a husband. They did not know that the dutiful daughter had dedicated herself to care for her parents in their old age. Forwardness she despised. I "can never respect any woman," she wrote, "who boldly seeks the attentions, or invades their province whose part it is to make advances, to legislate, and to bear rule."[32] But she would not have us think she was single for want of asking. "Sundry times, also, I came near being caught in the clerical net, but broke through."[33] One of these dangerous snares was probably the minister with whom during one winter she studied Hebrew; for the warm enthusiasm the book of *Jonah* inspired in her reflects more than an interest in Hebrew grammar. "The recreant prophet seemed to become a personal friend," she wrote. "Indeed, my indwelling with him was intense."[34]

But this scholarly person, together with an unnamed missionary and various other gentlemen darkly hinted of in vague numbers, men of "worth . . . and wealth, and mental culture, and the world's consideration,"[35] were rejected in favor of the "aged parents," the younger of whom was just forty-three. Lydia was making her way unobtrusively, but surely, into Hartford society. The elder people, charmed by the thoughtful ways of the pretty girl, sometimes forgot her humble origin. She was clever and amusing as well. At a meeting of the literary club in which everyone was to impersonate some famous character in the reign of Queen Anne, she was chosen for the Queen; and "the quiet humor with which she exhibited the stupidity and weakness of her British Majesty, afforded unbounded mirth and admiration to her friends around."[36] More than one of the writers whose names were to be household words in later years, "Peter Parley" and Whittier, for example, remembered with gratitude the kindly advice and encouragement Lydia Huntley gave them at this time.

As the school began its fourth year, she was just twenty-eight, an age at which matrimony began to seem unlikely. But, again in her own words, "the blind archer, though oft repulsed, and long held in subjection, bided his time." And when he chose to attack, it was through the graces of Charles Sigourney,* "a gentleman of strik-

* The accent is on the first syllable, the *g* hard.

ing physiognomy and the elegant manners of the olden school,'' whose wife had died a year before, leaving him with a son of eight and two younger daughters. Passing him each morning on the way to school, Miss Huntley looked her sympathy, while his ''deep-set and most expressive black eyes . . . spoke unutterable things.'' And when a letter came, ''a letter of touching eloquence and the fairest chirography,''[37] resistance was useless.

The son of a Boston merchant, Mr. Sigourney had ''been inured to habits of obedience, order, and application''[38] during a short residence in an English school, before he entered his father's store at the age of thirteen to serve his apprenticeship. On the turn of the century his father sent him to Hartford to set up for himself in the hardware business.

His personal appearance, if not forbidding, was at least one to repel familiarity. The forehead, high and broad, was surmounted by close-trimmed, spiky hair. The piercing eyes, set rather close, seemed smaller than they were through the old-fashioned, silver-rimmed spectacles, and together with the long, pointed nose gave his face the peculiar birdlike look common to near-sighted people. The extraordinarily high collar of the day, passing just below the ears and cutting the cheek to within an inch of the mouth, exaggerated the bitter expression of thin, tight lips.

He was hardly a romantic lover. The love of order and exactness that dominated his mind may, as his wife suggests, have arisen from a fondness for geometry. But precision alone does not nourish romance, and it was clearly his ruling passion. Lydia wrote:

His native taste for literature and the fine arts was carefully cherished. He was a critical judge of pictures, and drew archi-

Charles Sigourney

From *First Century of The Phoenix National Bank
of Hartford.*

tecturally with precision and elegance. He was fond of history
and the standard authors, but objected to the floating miscel-
lanies of the day, as furnishing no nutritive aliment to the
mind, and enervating its appetite for solidity. So elevated was
his theory, that he decried the use of newspapers for the young,
as tending to debase the style by bad models of composition,
and to weaken the retentive powers by reading what they did
not intend to remember, and what was not worthy of being remembered. He was watchful against new-coined words and in-
novations of the language, constantly referring to the large
edition of Dr. Johnson's Dictionary for etymology and shades
of signification.[39]

The Wadsworths, when they were consulted, adduced
many reasons, none of which were really needed, to per-
suade the fluttering schoolmistress, concluding—and perhaps echoing her thought—that the proposal "should be
viewed as a favoring providence of our Heavenly Bene-
factor."[40] Her mother and father, too, quite unaware of
her devotion to celibacy on their account, gladly gave
their consent. And on January 27, 1819, Lydia wrote in
her journal:

Last evening I promised to do all in my power to advance
the happiness of a man of the purest integrity, sensibility, and
piety. I surely anticipate improvement from intercourse with
his elegant and scientific mind, but cannot avoid shuddering at
my unfitness to fill the station his generosity has designated.[41]

One Sunday in April, Mr. Sigourney drove with her to
Norwich to be presented to the Huntleys. They sat apart
in austere dignity; and as she studied the lace on the
handkerchief Miss Wadsworth had given her, Lydia felt
just a little anxious about the "elegant and scientific
mind." Her simple country parents might not appreciate
the intellectual conversation on elevated subjects from

which Mr. Sigourney was never ''deterred by the impu-
tation of pedantry.''[42] The meeting proved much as she
feared. With Mr. Huntley, the fiancé naturally found little in common; but Lydia's mother, not many years older
than himself, made a more favorable impression, and was,
no doubt, visibly gratified at the prospect of a son-in-law.
Together the lovers admired the ''rural walks'' and land-
scape of Norwich, and when they parted, her future husband placed in her hands as a token of his esteem, a copy
of Wakefield's *Botany,* a small microscope, and eight
volumes of *Sir Charles Grandison,* which he commended
to her perusal.[43] If he hoped that she would notice any
resemblance between himself and that noblest of men, he
was to be disappointed; she read it as a duty, but it did
not interest her. Aside from diligent study of the *Botany,*
and the preparations for the wedding, the weeks were
broken only by the ''long, journalizing letters'' from Mr.
Sigourney, ''rich in description and philosophical remark, and redolent of the love-spell.''[44]

And when she stood before the altar on the sixteenth
of June, the same sentimental trance through which she
had viewed Madam Lathrop's funeral enwrapped her.
''What first restored full consciousness, was the blessing
of an old lady of ninety—Madam Lathrop, a connection
of my earliest benefactress—and the fervent glance of
her still lustrous black eye.''[45]

By the time they reached Hartford the forty-mile ride
had brought back her sense of reality. The sun was setting when they drew up before Mr. Sigourney's house,
where the two little stepdaughters stood as they had been
directed to greet their new mother. And as the last of
the wedding guests departed, the bells of North and
South churches, which she had heard fifteen years before

on her first visit to Hartford, were striking nine with alternate strokes, before joining their notes to tell the day of the month. One bell had "a deep, heavy tone, the other a melodious one; and their concord was like that of bass and treble in perfect harmony."[46]

Perfect harmony! She turned from the door, obedient to her husband's first request. The words she had written in her journal by the dim light of the morning came once more to her mind:

Blessed Trinity! endue me with such virtues and graces as my lot may require. May I move in the untried sphere that awaits me with the humility of a Christian and the benevolence of an angel . . .[47]

CHAPTER TWO

THE KITCHEN IN PARNASSUS

EVERYONE agreed that Lydia had made a splendid marriage. Mr. Sigourney's grave dignity and blunt way of expressing his opinion made him rather difficult at times; but he was prosperous and respected by all who knew him, and a girl of her origin could hardly expect more. The end of the war in 1816 had released the long-pent-up foreign trade, and the merchants were reaping great profits. Every few days a large schooner would pick her way up the river among hundreds of sloops, brigs, flatboats, and rafts, to lie in a thicket of masts along the Hartford wharf unloading their cargoes. Advertisements would presently appear in the papers describing anvils, sadirons, jewelry and watches, tea trays, candle snuffers, horse fleams, scissors, carpets, spectacles, bodkins, jew's-harps, warming pans, sleeve buttons, fine skates from Holland, molasses for the distilleries, brass letters and other trimmings for coffins—all consigned to the merchants, who would soon distribute them throughout the length and breadth of Connecticut and a hundred miles to the north. The hardware business did not occupy all of Mr. Sigourney's attention, however; he was identified with all good causes, finding time to serve as warden of Christ Church, president of the Phœnix Bank, and trustee of Trinity (then Washington) College.

From his own plans he presently built a fine house in what, at that time, was open country. Crowded as it now is by warehouses and factories, its sloping lawns cut by the ugly railroad embankment, the house still retains the quiet dignity of a century ago. Daniel Wadsworth, wrapped in a series of capes, which he affected partly from artistic fancy and partly from an exaggerated fear of drafts, came riding out in his big yellow coach, fitted with a stove and chimney, from which the smoke was pouring.[48] As he surveyed the stately portico, the lofty windows rising from the floor, the marble fireplaces, the fine spiral staircase, he felt a tingle of self-gratulatory pleasure to think that through his guidance the daughter of Aunt Lathrop's gardener was placed at the head of this magnificent establishment.

Her predecessor had been "a model of excellence";[49] and Lydia, wise enough to avoid competing too soon with her memory, assumed the humility she had prayed for. When the "aristocracy" called, she considered it a demonstration of the respect due her husband. Nor were these the only occasions when she could practice humility. Living in the household was Miss Carter, a sister of the first Mrs. Sigourney, who had looked after the children during their mother's illness, and was no more eager to surrender their charge and affection than any other spinster of forty-two would be in like circumstances. There were many chances for collision in becoming mistress of a house that had been running for sixteen years; but Lydia assumed her place gracefully. The stepchildren were soon reciting the lessons in geography, history, and Bible that she simplified for their years. On

fair days it might be in the little summerhouse with its
bright new weather vane inscribed *Ut ventus vita,* or, as
a special favor, at the ''Hermitage,'' a rustic shelter built
on a large oak over the stream that flowed through the
lower grounds. Knitting needles were clicking whenever
her hands were not otherwise occupied, turning out incredible quantities of gloves and stockings. One early
domestic triumph that brought words of praise from Mr.
Sigourney was a pair of mazarine-blue bombazine pantaloons trimmed with white pearl buttons; but it is doubtful if the eight-year-old stepson who had to wear them
shared her satisfaction. Relations with the neighbors
were gradually established. Learning that before her illness the late Mrs. Sigourney had intended to give
''Aunt'' Polly Lawrence a new bonnet, she sent one, and
with it a shawl, some muslin for caps, and a book.

One summer Mr. Sigourney took her to Boston to see
his relatives; but she was never very intimate with them.
She much preferred the quiet days at Sachem's Head,
whither he drove his own horse after the bank elections.
Here, with reading and needlework, she relaxed and
rested from the eager strain of her first years in ''fash-
ionable society,'' while her husband swam in the cool
waters of the Sound or went off, hammer in hand, on long
geological expeditions, collecting feldspars and crystals.

But, advantageous as it seemed to the world, marriage
shattered Lydia's dream of supporting her parents by
her writings. Mr. Sigourney, to be sure, was not averse
to literature as a social accomplishment, an elegant pas-
time; but he was insistent that it should remain so. Soon
after the wedding she was compelled to discontinue a
good-natured anonymous satire called *The Square Table,*
when her identity was in danger of discovery. Perhaps it

The Charles Sigourney House, Hartford

By Permission of The Connecticut Historical Society.

was to compensate for this that her husband added notes
and helped her publish, also anonymously, her Indian
epic, *Traits of the Aborigines*. The reviewer of *Moral
Pieces* had urged her to try "some more considerable undertaking" and suggested that the legends of the Indians
offered opportunities greater than Scott found in the bor-
der wars. With no apparent diffidence, she had set to
work, and finished the two hundred pages by 1817; but
they were not published until 1822.

After reading this poem, one feels a little as Agnes
Repplier did of *Uncle Tom's Cabin:* that an oppression
which could develop such sterling characters ought never
to have been removed. Mrs. Sigourney's Indians all possess to a marked degree the virtues of friendship, gratitude, reverence for age, and piety; and the similarity of
their sacrifices to those of the ancient Hebrews indicates
to her that they are perhaps descended from the lost
tribes of Israel. However that may be, no patriarch could
have behaved more honorably to Capt. John Smith, who,
after prolonged negotiations with the Indians

> tastes the captive's lot
> And borne in triumph sees the royal tent
> Of Worowocomoco. There enthron'd
> Sat great Powhatan,[50]

a most chivalrous monarch, who, while dooming him to
death, "gaily strives" to cheer his captive with a feast.
When he is led to the block, no shout,

> no taunting hiss
> Broke on the deep solemnity; it seem'd
> A deed of stern, reluctant policy,
> Averting evil, not avenging hate.[51]

Even the grim executioners share their leader's delicacy
and, clubs in air, "await the signal with averted face."
Then Pocahontas, who has seemed "to shrink as the
Mimosa," clasps his head:

> "Now let the death stroke fall!"
> Boldly she cried, "for ere it reach that head
> This shall be crush'd." The warriors' uprais'd arm,
> For execution bar'd in vigorous strength
> Unconsciously declin'd, and deep respect
> Ev'n for a child, wander'd with soft'ning trace
> O'er their hard features. That unwonted sight
> The monarch could not brook; his soul was mov'd
> To mark his daughter's bearing, and he bade
> To loose the prisoner's bonds, and loud exclaim'd,
> "Rise! and be free."[52]

This and other less familiar tales out of Schoolcraft
and Heckewelder are set forth with a profusion of classical allusion and biblical simile that must have made
Mr. Wadsworth marvel. If the Indians could know of
Cambyses, Xerxes, Caligula, and Nero, Lydia declares,

> they would reject the charge
> That they alone, above all men, were stain'd
> With dark barbarity.[53]

In defense of their methods of warfare she asks why it is
any worse to hide behind a tree than a palisade.

> O'er the tow'rs
> Of lofty Ilion, wreck'd by Grecian wiles,
> Why does the dazzled eye prolong its gaze
> In breathless interest, yet avert its glance
> Disgusted, and indignant, at the scenes
> Of Indian stratagem?[54]

Indulging in poetic vision, she paints in the last canto a rosy picture of the Christian Indians:

> A happy band I see,
> Bending intently o'er the sacred page,
> With sudden comprehension, while glad tears
> Unconscious start.[55]

There follows an impassioned appeal for the support of missionaries:

> Full many a name
> Which Fashion flaunting in her gilded car
> Heeds not amid her pomp, is register'd
> In the Lamb's book of life. . . .[56]
> To you, their hands
> They raise, imploring. Tears of anguish stain
> Their haggard features. Timidly they lead
> Their untaught children, asking you to grant
> Pity and comfort.[57]

And the final argument, urging conversion of the Indians as the only means of making the West safe for settlers, should certainly have given the book a broad utilitarian appeal.

It was Mr. Sigourney's idea to interpret the text with elaborate notes so that the volume would be useful as a reference work on the Indians. One example will show with what deadly effect the combination was made. Some of the squaw's occupations, Mrs. Sigourney says, were to cultivate the maize,

> The swelling legume, and that tub'rous root
> Which in their clay-built cells, the hardy sons
> Of emerald Erin bless.[58]

Now, turning to the notes, the reader is gratified to learn that "America presented Europe with the Solanum tuberosum" or common potato, and, again, that "according to Morabelli's analysis of the Zea mays," it contains some twenty or more chemical compounds, whose names are duly listed!

Yet somehow the book was not popular. In 1822 when it appeared, the Cherokee Nation had just announced a firm resolution not to cede any more land to the Government, which, under pressure from the state of Georgia, had coolly disregarded the earlier treaties one after another. The Society for the Civilization and General Advancement of the Indian Tribes founded a few months before had been rebuffed by John Adams, Jefferson, and Marshall, who thought it an interference with government policy, and had made little progress in obtaining justice for the Red Man. The newspapers advertised Indian lands for sale, and from time to time, with unmixed glee, reported glorious victories: Four hundred brave soldiers fall upon an Indian village and kill all of its sixty-eight inhabitants! As an appeal to charity the poem fell on rather stony soil.

Mrs. Sigourney, however, followed her own precepts. Packages of improving books—perhaps with a few copies of *Traits of the Aborigines*—were soon on their way to the "Untutored Indian." One chief to whom, on hearing that he was addicted to alcohol, she had written a personal exhortation, replied through an interpreter that he realized he was an ignorant heathen, walking in the dark, but stoutly maintained that he had "left off whiskey"[59] two years before. The Charity Society organized during the first years of Miss Huntley's school was still holding regular meetings with thirty or forty young ladies in at-

tendance, all busily sewing useful little things for their
Forest Brothers. At one of their gatherings Mrs. Sigourney read a letter from an Indian expressing thanks to
the young ladies by

whos liberreal hand Choctaw Children are greatly benifted. It
is not me that can tell who is brote to believe the trugth. I
therefore will say nothing on the Subject. I am ashamed to tell
you, that my Brother McKee have left off Religion of Lord Je-
sus Christ and he has take the path of the prodical son and he
is gone, and I do not know that he will return to his father.[60]

His report on the physical welfare of the tribe is more
assuring; but the dazzling light of redemption that shone
so brightly on the Charitable Society had not reached
even the most eager of converts.

With much confused of face I must tell you, dear friend, I
am still in the dark as to the things of eternal happiness beyond the grave. I do not blame no other being but myself on
account of my wickedness my rebullious stoborn heart to the
laws of God, that I am left in the dark o, wicked man I am. I
need your praier and the prayers of your Christian Brethren
and Sestirs tell them to pray for me. We Choctaws will still
look toward you my Christian friend for help Constanly.

Toward her they did not look in vain. The boxes of useful
articles were dispatched regularly with patient letters of
exhortation and kindly interest. As a further inspiration,
she asked one chief to choose a recently converted maiden
from his tribe to bear the name of Lydia Sigourney, if
there were not already one in the town.

When Lafayette came to Hartford in 1824, Mr. Wadsworth, who was in charge of the arrangements for his reception, took pains that his *protégée* should share in the
glory. The reception was like all the others to which La-

fayette was subjected. He rode under triumphal arches, reviewed the troops, shook hands with veterans of the Revolution, dined with the city fathers, and hurried on his way. There was this difference, however, in the Hartford welcome: On the spot where the reviewers stood, Washington had first met Rochambeau at the head of the French army; in the Wadsworth mansion just across the street they had planned the siege of Yorktown. "This surely was classic ground," said the *Courant*.[61]

After the review Lafayette alighted at the State House, passing between rows of children from the schools of the city, marshaled in regular lines. His interest was perhaps quickened by the wide sashes they all wore over their shoulders, bearing the hearty legend, "Nous Vous Aimons La Fayette," the refrain of a poem written for the occasion by Mrs. Sigourney, and presented to the hero as soon as he entered the building.

> Welcome thou to Freedom's clime,
> Glorious Hero! Chief sublime!
> Garlands bright for thee are wreath'd,
> Vows of filial ardour breath'd,
> Veteran's cheeks with tears are wet,
> "Nous vous aimons La Fayette."
>
> .   .   .   .   .   .
>
> Brandywine, whose currents roll'd
> Proud with blood of heroes bold,
> *That* our Country's debt shall tell
> *That* our gratitude shall swell,
> Infant breasts thy wounds regret,
> "Nous vous aimons La Fayette."
>
> Sires, who sleep in glory's bed,
> Sires, whose blood for us was shed,

Taught us, when our knee we bend,
With the prayer thy name to blend:
Shall we e'er such charge forget?
No!—"NOUS AIMONS LA FAYETTE."

WHEN our blooming cheeks shall fade,
Pale with time, or sorrow's shade,
When our clustering tresses fair
Frosts of wintry age shall wear,
E'en till Memory's sun be set,
"NOUS VOUS AIMONS LA FAYETTE."[62]

The reception within the State House was given over entirely to the ladies; and among the hundreds whom he took by the hand in the most affectionate manner, none received more compliments than the charming Mrs. Sigourney who had written the touching verses.

His last visit was to Mr. Wadsworth's house, whither he came on foot to inspect the sash he had worn at the battle of Brandywine and later presented to General Swift of Cornwall. Here again he met the vivacious Mrs. Sigourney, and assured her that he would take her little poem home to his daughters, or listened, perhaps, with interest to the part her venerable father had played in the Revolution. Then, having taken leave of the ladies and gentlemen, he was attended to the boat for New York.

A trip to Virginia in 1825 supplied Lydia with subjects for scores of new poems. Mr. Sigourney's grand manner was at its best. They went to stare at old Jefferson; they called on the Madisons; they dined with President Adams; they visited all the historical spots.[63] Yet a dull monotony pervades the verses in which Lydia celebrated everything from the tomb of Washington's mother to the thundershower that overtook them one afternoon.

"Hail! holy dome!" is the invariable apostrophe to any
sort of building—Jamestown Church, Mount Vernon, the
University of Virginia—regardless of architectural type.
But when she came home, the Hartford papers were
grateful for the poems, printing them with her maiden
signature, "H."

About this time America, led by republican sympathy
and Lord Byron's magnificent espousal of the cause, was
beginning to display an interest in the Greek Revolution.
Missionary zeal, stirred by two decades of revivals, gazed
impatiently across the ocean at this new field for the triumph of the Gospel. "How delightful to overspread
Greece with bibles," exclaimed one enthusiast, "and to
furnish her the chosen heralds of salvation!"[64] Mrs.
Sigourney threw herself into the struggle. As secretary
of the Executive Committee of Ladies she canvassed the
town for subscriptions; and staid merchants who had
been scandalously disloyal when their own Government
was at war with England a dozen years before, cheerfully abetted revolution abroad. Contributions poured in.
With a hundred yards of cloth donated by the college
youths, the girls of Miss Beecher's school made useful
garments for their suffering Greek sisters. The ladies of
the Charitable Society turned with Lydia from the contemplation of the Aborigines to "that Classick Clime"
where Byron fell. Poor Byron! A wicked man he had undoubtedly been. But surely Missolonghi atoned for all.
Mrs. Sigourney put her view of the matter into verse:

> Cold rests his heart within thy hallow'd bowers,
> And Helle's maiden's wreathe its shrine with flowers.—
> —Genius of Greece! who drank his latest sigh,
> Raise toward the Queen of Isle's thy mourning eye . . .

Say, "for *my sake* thy wayward bard forgive,
Since, bound with mine, his deathless name shall live;
Breathe o'er his filial urn one sorrowing sigh,
And in his glory let his frailties die."[65]

When everything was ready to be sent to the ship, Mrs. Sigourney wrote her *Letter to the Ladies of Greece from the Ladies of Hartford.*

SISTERS AND FRIENDS,—

From the years of childhood your native clime has been the theme of our admiration: together with our brothers and our husbands we early learned to love the country of Homer, Aristides, of Solon, and of Socrates. That enthusiasm which the glory of ancient Greece enkindled in our bosoms, has preserved a fervent friendship for her descendants. . . .

Sisters and friends, our hearts bleed for you . . . The poor among us have given according to their ability, and our little children have cheerfully aided, that some of you and your children might have bread to eat, and raiment to put on. Could you but behold the faces of our little ones brighten, and their eyes sparkle with joy, while they give up their holidays, that they might work with their needles for Greece . . . it would cheer for a moment the darkness and misery of your lot. . . .

Sisters and friends, we extend across the ocean our hands to you in the fellowship of Christ. We pray that His Cross and the banner of your land may rise together over the Crescent and the Minaret—that your sons may hail the freedom of ancient Greece restored, and build again the waste places which the oppressor hath trodden down; and that you, admitted once more to the felicities of home, may gather from past perils and adversities, a brighter wreath for the kingdom of Heaven.

And then a real Greek came to town. Demetrius Stamatiades, a young native of Samos, sent to America to be educated, was given work in the hardware store and taken to board at the Sigourney's house. Excitement ran

high. The young ladies begged him to recite one of the
patriotic orations of Tricoussi which he had translated.[66]
They began to study modern Greek. Even sedate Mr.
Sigourney caught the fever and rose early in the morning to be shown how closely modern Greek resembled
that of Pericles, from which it had never been divided
"except in the heads of American *savants*." And even
ten years later when Demetrius had returned home, there
was still mild enthusiasm over the long letters beginning
"My Dear American Mother," expressing regret that the
death of the Sultan made it impossible to obtain the autograph she had asked for, but sending, perhaps, a pair of
Turkish slippers for "my little sister Mary" or a few
bits of Mosaic from the dome of St. Sophia for little Andrew—the two children born to the Sigourneys while he
was in Hartford.[67]

Americans, complacent of salvation, watched the
morning light breaking over "kingdoms wide that sat in
darkness."[68]

> We are living, we are dwelling
> In a grand and awful time,[69]

they told each other solemnly. Greece was only one act of
the great drama. From evangelists in Burma, in Siam, in
Africa, in China, from Greenland to the South Seas,
wherever

> The heathen, in his blindness
> Bows down to wood and stone,[70]

appeals of the most urgent kind came to Mrs. Sigourney
and the Charitable Young Ladies. At home the blind, the
deaf and dumb, the insane, those in prisons and reform

schools were all crying for help and guidance. With the great bundles of garments Mrs. Sigourney always sent off improving books or temperance tracts. In one package for Wethersfield she put a special *Prisoners' Evening Hymn: Written for the Females in the Connecticut State Prison,* who must have been uncommonly edified to sing :

> The way of wickedness is hard,
> Its bitter fruits we know,
> Shame in this world is its reward
> And in the future, woe.[71]

An even more pressing appeal was for money to support her parents. Mr. Huntley was now approaching eighty, and his household required more than was supplied by his soldier's pension and what his daughter could save out of pin money. Mr. Sigourney was generous; but, in truth, his affluence had been somewhat exaggerated. A drygoods business in which he was partner failed the year of his marriage; the brisk hardware trade that followed the war, inviting optimism, had quickly passed; the salary from the bank never exceeded $700 a year; and his house had cost more than he estimated. Economy, though nothing new to Lydia, was not so easy there as in the Norwich cottage; but she recorded every penny in her account book, and, to the further discomfort of master Charles, arranged to "prolong the existence of all garments, by repair or transmigration."[72] Finally, in 1827, she gathered up the "poetical fruits" of the Virginia trip, culled from her old journals a few more variations on the Death of a Venerable Benefactress, added some less personal numbers like the *Lines: On the Translation of Milton into the Language of Iceland by Tholasken, a Native Poet,*[73] and packed them all off to S. G.

Goodrich (Peter Parley), a former member of the Hartford "literary circle," now a printer in Boston. The proceeds from this volume, such as they were, she devoted to her parents. And from now on the poetical "effusions" were sent mostly to newspapers and magazines that paid for them, with brief little notes informing the editor that she has more inquiries for "simple pieces of this nature than leisure to produce them," and would like them returned, if they cannot be used. More than twenty periodicals were accepting them regularly in 1830.

A collection of biographies, abridged originally for use in the school, produced "a small stipend"; and when a second volume was in preparation, her friend, Theodore Dwight, Jr., an editor in Brooklyn, urged her to put her name to the work, all the books since her marriage having appeared anonymously. It would increase sales, she agreed.

But I am not able to consult either your wishes or my own, since a decree more imperative exists. My husband has often expressed his decided aversion to this step, even when he warmly patronized my intellectual pursuits, and now that he has become their opposer, it would of course, create violent displeasure. It is my duty in this case, as well as in all others, to consult his feelings as far as it may be in my power, without utterly burying in the earth those "few talents" for which I am responsible to their Giver and Judge.[74]

And she maintained an anonymity so complete that even Mr. Sigourney himself was not to know of the book; her letters are full of elaborate arrangements for getting proof sheets through friends and of the danger of "multiplying confidantes."[75]

Some of the poetical pieces, on the contrary, had been signed; but when Dwight again urged a volume of them

under her name, she explained that the "production of
fugitive pieces, is not . . . viewed with the same degree
of dislike, as the gathering & laying them in a tangible
form before the ordeal of the publick." But the collection
he suggests would, she feared, "be disagreeable to those,
whom it is my duty to conciliate."[76]

To conciliate! Ten years before she had shuddered at
her unfitness "to fill the station his generosity had designated." Ten years before she had resigned forever the
career of writer, and recorded in her journal the pang it
caused:

> Thou too, my harp! and can it be,
> That I must bid adieu to thee? . . .
> Oh! dearer far than words can tell,
> My wild, my mountain-harp—*farewell!*[77]

And now she is conciliating "those whose wishes duty
binds me to consult."[78]

Within a year, however, conciliation and duty alike
succumbed to economic pressure. In the spring of 1833
Letters to Young Ladies, By a Lady was published at her
own risk, with the copyright taken in Mr. Huntley's
name. "I wish to avoid notoriety, with regard to it," she
wrote, ". . . but if it should be fixed on me, I have no
disposition to deny it."[79] Of course, it was fixed on her,
and she avowed it with becoming modesty and promptly
put her name on the later editions. The book sold amaz-
ingly and the advertising it gave her trebled the demand
for her writings. In that year and the next, nine volumes
came from her pen, hack work all of it: another historical
abridgment, an obituary volume, a pacifist-propaganda
story, a report of the Female Beneficent Society, *How To
Be Happy*, a volume of tales, and two fat volumes of po-

etry. Of a total of nearly 1,500 pages, at least 1,000 were written within the year.

I will tell *you* still further [she wrote to Dwight], that as my husband has not recently been prosperous in his business, I have felt it my duty to aid him, by pursuing more as a trade, what had previously been only a recreation or solace. It is now considerably more than a year, since I have supplied all my expenses of clothing, charity, literature &c, beside paying the wages of a woman, who relieves me a part of the day from household care, and I take great pleasure in doing it. I also educate my little children, & take unspeakable delight in their daily lessons.[80]

Literature had become her trade, and she gloried in it. A huge new reading public had appeared, thirsty for periodicals, and crying like newborn Gargantua for drink. Mrs. Sigourney with her dilute, saccharine verses capitalized this thirst, and made it her principal source of income. In newspapers from Maine to South Carolina, from Baltimore to Cincinnati, the poems were printed, until her name was known everywhere. Like *Letters to Young Ladies* many of them were composed for the girls of Miss Huntley's school, and their highly moral and didactic tone recommended them to the great number of readers who were not yet certain that it was right to enjoy any literature but the Bible. Brought up in the conservative atmosphere of Norwich and Hartford, Mrs. Sigourney had an inevitably restricted view of life; but her very limitations were responsible for her success with the enormous new public made up largely of women with views like her own.

Swarms of annuals and gift books, crowding thick upon each other, were engaged in suffocating competition. All of them—from the "aristocratic" *Keepsake* of the Countess of Blessington to the *Glasgow Infant School Annual,* from the perennial *Token* to the humble *Harebell*—all of them accepted her poems, and paid for them or got no more. To an illustrious and popular contributor the price was sometimes $10.00 for a piece of ordinary length; the usual rate was only $2.00 a page, though some paid as much as $5.00 a stanza. The *Gift* sent her $100 for three or four somewhat longer poems to fill about twenty pages.[81] The general rule was to get as much as possible, and she developed a fine technique for doing it.

Soon publishers were bidding against each other for the privilege of simply using her name as editor of their magazines. From 1840 to 1842 Louis Godey, in the pages of whose *Lady's Book,* Mr. Minnigerode believed "were to be found the habitually unremunerated prose and verse" of the Fabulous Forties,[82] paid $500 a year to have her name on the title-page. When the editor of the rival *Ladies' Companion* assured his readers that "her engagements in other quarters" would not interfere with regular contributions to the *Companion,* Godey protested vehemently, declaring that the appearance of her name "on any other publication than mine would completely neutralize the benefit I expect to receive."[83] With every mail money came dribbling in, fitfully at first and from many sources, then in steadily increasing amounts, until it became a dependable income. She was beset with proposals for longer works. The *Southern Literary Messenger* wanted a biographical sketch of John Marshall, one of the lions who had escaped her in 1825.[84] A biography of her prototype, Mrs. Hemans, "formed on the basis of Chorley's view of the poetess, collated with those of other writers," was entirely superseded when the Edinburgh edition of the *Works* arrived, and she threw it aside and "prepared" another from the new authorities for the sum of $100.[85]

Had she possessed a poetically fertile mind, it would still have been physically impossible to supply the demand for new poems. She fell back on the old formulas, Reverence for Age, Resignation, Death—particularly Death— the death of infants, dying boys' last bequests, the death of consumptive girls, of missionaries in Burma and Liberia, of poets and lunatics, artists and sailors, college students and deaf-dumb-and-blind girls. Deep grief, she declared in soothing sibilants,

seeks to be alone, that it may meditate without interruption, on the loved and lost. . . . Over this season of solitude, perchance too long or too gloomily cherished, the sigh of sacred poesy steals without startling. Culling the blessed words of Scripture, she lays them, like dewy flowers, in the lap of the weeper, and departs.[86]

Every subject, no matter how remote it might seem, provided some lesson "to teach the mournful moralist to die."[87]

Most of the poems served at least twice, going the rounds from paper to paper without change. Always within a few months or even days of their first publication, they would be gathered up with a few more of the endless lines on the Ancient Benefactress and a dozen pages of new verses, and dispatched to a publisher, who would plead for more. She was forever "discovering" an article written some time before, or "decimating" a pile of manuscripts in the attic to produce volume after volume of three hundred pages. The pious account of her associate in the Norwich school, written for the family in 1816, was soon condensed into a magazine article and still later made into chapters for *Scenes in My Native*

Land and *Letters to My Pupils.* Trading on her school
experience, she turned out a *Boy's Reading Book* and a
Girl's Reading Book at a royalty of ten cents per copy
and, by a skilful insistence on their unimpeachable morality, got them adopted in such schools as the West Hoboken Institute.[88] In ten days she wrote *How To Be
Happy,* of which thousands were sold. And she furthered
the circulation of all her books by sending bundles of
them, after careful inquiry, to booksellers in Albany or
Richmond and collecting her own commission.[89]

By 1836 she had become one of the most successful
writers for annuals, and when the Rev. Dr. Bedell died,
she was persuaded without much effort to take up his
work as editor of the *Religious Souvenir.* With characteristic energy she began at once the task of soliciting articles. She had never betrayed the slightest hesitation
about writing to utter strangers; and now she dispatched
hundreds of letters to all the writers and painters of
reputation, inviting "effusions" and illustrations. Most
of the artists replied, like Washington Allston,[90] that annuals were too small to reproduce their work well, though
S. F. B. Morse did supply a mediocre view of Athens
around which Mrs. Sigourney wrote a story of forty
pages. From England only Mrs. Opie and Shelton Mackenzie (to whose own annual Mrs. Sigourney was a
contributor) sent articles. In America, Holmes declared
that the cares and labors of his profession "would soon
destroy, at least for a time, the inclination to verse which
has been one of my failings,"[91] and R. H. Dana, accepting her flattery, politely declined to furnish anything.[92]
When the *Souvenir* appeared, just before Christmas,
1838, the principal articles were by Mrs. Hale, Miss
Gould, Miss Sedgwick, Mrs. Embury, Miss Lynch, and

Mrs. Stowe, then just beginning, like Mrs. Sigourney, to write for a living. Daniel Wadsworth was gratified to see amidst this female galaxy his description of Niagara. The missionary field had its share of space. The Rev. C. S. Stewart, a chaplain in the navy, furnished a picture of a Marquesan cottage, and filled thirty pages with the virtues of his late wife. The Rev. John Williams wrote of Polycarp; and Stamatiades, signing himself "M. D.," sent a long account of the island of Syra. Nearly 100 pages of the volume were written by the gifted editor herself. The "Tale of Ancient Athens" (destined later to appear as "Myrtis" in the volume of that name) and a description of Norwich (parts of which had already appeared in 1824), were signed; but several other articles, bearing the initials "C." or "H." and betraying her touch, are perhaps explained by the flat rate allowed by the publishers of $2.00 a page.[93]

She brought out the *Souvenir* for the next year in much the same style; but the weighty correspondence occupied more time than the demands of other editors left her, and she ended the work here. With her usual thrift, however, she secured the stereotype plates, and for years afterward the books were occasionally reissued under various titles.

Mr. Sigourney surveyed with Olympian disdain the litter of manuscript, the ink-stained fingers, and the avalanche of correspondence. Care had deepened the hard lines about his mouth. He was only sixty; but his mind had lost its resilience, congealed. Swift-moving progress had passed him by. His wife, thirteen years younger than he, the gardener's daughter he had so graciously lifted to his own rank, was a thorn in his flesh, openly rebellious, disregarding his wishes by screeching his patrician name aloud in every cheap journal at home and abroad. Financial trouble was hard enough to bear without advertising. His two daughters, elegant young ladies educated at Miss Beecher's and the celebrated Madame Chegary's boarding school in New York, assured him of their sympathy by treating their stepmother with scant deference. Still, her own children gave her solace. Little Mary copied out many a page of verses; while Andrew, standing at her side, offered with comprehension beyond his years greater comfort from the depths of grave, violet eyes.

The buoyant spirit of expansion that was in the air left Mr. Sigourney unstirred. In the bank younger, more adventurous men found the methods of 1816 inadequate for the business of 1836. There had been friction and opposition. Mr. Sigourney had opened, it was said, a private letter addressed to Mr. Beach, the cashier, and divulged its contents; and after urging Beach's removal in a pamphlet[94] (promptly repudiated by the Directors as inaccurate), he was forced to resign. Mr. Beach produced a counterblast;[95] Mr. Sigourney answered with a pedantic display of Latin and florid rhetoric:

As a famished dog rushes upon a dropped joint of meat, [he sneered,] so does the hired and paid writer of Mr. Beach's pamphlet . . . rush upon this unfortunate mistake, fortunate indeed for him, and torture from it three pages of valiant and victorious refutation.[96]

But with all his eloquence he won no proxies for the next election. The incident had another effect. Mr. Beach, in a happier day, had been Andrew's godfather; and in attacking him Mr. Sigourney widened the gulf that had opened between Lydia and himself.

In 1838 they had to leave the lovely house on the hill

and move to one in High Street. The change, severing the ties of eighteen years, was a blow to pride rather than comfort; for those years in "the dear retreat, the Eden-home,"[97] as Mrs. Sigourney was soon calling it, had not been quite the unalloyed bliss that she pretended. Such a sorrow was material for poetry, however, and all her correspondents were elaborately informed of the melancholy removal. "But how soon shall we all be obliged to remove . . . to the dark & narrow house, appointed for all living," the everlasting house of the grave, replied a missionary in Greece,[98] of whom she inquired why His Majesty the King had never thanked her for the books she sent him. Within a month the *Mother's Magazine*[99] published a moral tale of a merchant who returned home one evening with the news that he had lost his whole fortune. "We can no longer keep our carriage. We must leave this large house." Mrs. Sigourney herself plays the heroine bravely. "The servants were dismissed. Pictures and plate, rich carpets and furniture, were sold, and she who had been so long the mistress of the mansion, shed no tear." The only difference is that, far from being surprised by a sudden announcement, Mrs. Sigourney in reality had been economizing for seventeen years and, during the last six, had even been contributing to the household expenses.[100]

Mr. Sigourney's daughters both married in 1839, leaving their stepmother without regret; now their father's only ally was his son Charles, a thin, sallow person of twenty-five. Mr. Sigourney was withdrawing into himself more and more, and could no longer be persuaded to show himself in the society he was once so fond of. If he had seen it, how heartily he would have echoed the sentiment of Mrs. Phelps's letter to Lydia: "There is great danger that injustice may be done in the public mind to a gentleman when his wife makes herself conspicuous. We must do all we can to prevent this.''[101] She was thinking, perhaps, of her sister, Emma Willard, founder of the Troy Female Seminary, whose dashing second husband at their wedding dinner a month before had asked his wife for money to pay the bill. Lydia had known Mrs. Willard since the days when they labored together for Greek relief; they had exchanged views on education; and now they confided to each other their disillusion with matrimony. ''I dare not write you by mail except in a guarded way,'' Mrs. Willard says in a letter intrusted to one of the teachers in Troy, who was coming to Hartford.

. . . *You* I know would sympathize with me in many things— In some respects you could not from experience know what I had to suffer—in others my case presented less difficulties than yours—for I had no children to bind me to him, but rather affectionate children to receive me if I left him—but you have two step daughters—I had one. . . . You verily thought once you had friends in yours and so I thought of mine.[102]

Mrs. Sigourney could sympathize with Mrs. Willard by letter; but she had no intention of following her before the Connecticut Legislature asking a divorce. Mr. Sigourney, precise, passionless, could never be guilty of the indiscretion Mrs. Willard's husband committed in taking Mrs. Hale to a Harvard Commencement.[103] And, besides, the inviolable sanctity of the home was one of Mrs. Sigourney's constant themes, one in which she honestly believed. So she swallowed whatever disappointment marriage had brought, and eased her mind by tinting matrimony in rosy colors for others in such pious works as *Whisper to a Bride,* a chaste little volume bound in white watered silk and stamped with gilt cupids. We read:

A married man should have his true pre-eminence. . . .[104] When the romance beginneth to depart, and the gilding on the picture of young life is tarnished, be not startled or dejected, but call forth the good sense that taketh things as they are, and the sweet patience that winneth the victory.[105]

It is uncertain whether she practiced sweet patience consistently at home; but with her publishers she displayed a persistent sharpness of business dealing that was scarcely to be expected from a poetess. Percentages figure largely in plans for her books.

Not that I am mercenary [she explained to Dwight], but my time for writing is gathered by piece-meal, & as its avails are the only means by which I can connect myself with the ever-soliciting & noble charities of the day, I am induced to exhibit a regard for money, which I think is not inherent.[106]

By 1839 her income was large enough to give her a feeling of prosperity. Little Andrew acquired no pantaloons by "transmigration," but walked proudly to church beside his mother, dressed in a green merino jacket with scallops of black velvet at the belt, white pleated frill at the neck, and short white trousers.[107] The Muse who had smiled so benignly upon her efforts deserved a fitter temple than the little parlor in High Street; and, inclosing a book, of course, Mrs. Sigourney wrote to Ithiel Town, the famous New Haven architect, for his idea of a library to be added to the house.

If but one story [he replied], it might easily admit a study with a neatly ornamented ceiling in *gothic compartments,* in imitation of *oak-work* . . . and a little additional gothic window of *stained-glass* . . . placed high up in yᵉ gable . . .

would produce a very pleasing effect, especially in this little haunt of yᵉ Muses, where their inspirations to a favorite, as heretofore, would combine, in a high degree, the *good* and the *useful*, with the most lively and pleasing combinations of fancy.[108]

That was perhaps the secret of her success, combining the good and the useful, she thought, as she carefully tied off the last of two pairs of silk stockings knit (while composing verses) for the exhibition of the American Institute for the Encouragement of Manufactures.[109] And when the last New Year's verse had gone to the magazines, the last gift volume was sent, the elegiac poems written as requested for the "owner of a canary-bird, which had accidentally been starved to death," and for the father of the young child "drowned in a barrel of swine's food"[110] —then she opened her journal and summed up the year's achievement. Her pen had grown more facile since 1835, when she recorded "some degree of compunction that two months, with the exception of claims of correspondence and contributions to periodicals, should have been expended on a work of such trifling extent as one hundred and twenty-two pages."[111] Adding the items slowly, she totaled up and entered the number of calls paid, visits received, volumes read, garments made, and stockings knit, and in the same column the pages of prose and lines of poetry written during the year.[112] To her they all represented much the same sort of toil, and she saw no incongruity in classifying them together. Had not the great Maria Edgeworth commended her ability to write poems on the spur of the moment? "Gray could not— Addison could not. Mrs. Sigourney's friends will doubtless be ready to bear testimony that she can."[113] Susceptible to such equivocal flattery, Mrs. Sigourney loved to repeat the comment. But she was not altogether deceived about the quality of her work. "If there is any kitchen in Parnassus," she wrote toward the end of her life, "my Muse has surely officiated there as a woman of all work, and an aproned waiter."[114]

CHAPTER THREE

PLEASANT MEMORIES OF PLEASANT LANDS

"IF there be a spot on earth which angels might long to visit, and where they might fondly linger, it is the loving Christian family."[115] This one sentence from *The Family Circle,* a gift book to which Mrs. Sigourney was a contributor, will serve to disclose the aura of sentimental sanctity that hung in the nineteenth century about the subject of marriage. Finding the problem of family relations too difficult, the moralists of the time, gentlemen of the old school, heaped scorn on the pioneers of the feminist movement and invoked religion to maintain the *status quo*. The secret of domestic happiness, one of them wrote, "lies folded up in the leaves of the Bible,"[116] that is to say, in St. Paul's advice to the Corinthians and Ephesians of the first century.

The domestic constitution is a divine institute, [he continues]. God formed it himself. . . . When directed as it should be, every family has a sacred character, inasmuch as the head of it acts the part of both prophet and priest of the household, by instructing them in the knowledge, and leading them in the worship of God; while at the same time, he discharges the duties of a king by supporting a system of order, subordination, and discipline.[117]

As another writer stated it: "Home is the palace of the husband and the father. He is the monarch of that little empire, wearing a crown that is the gift of heaven."[118]

But in reality this attitude toward woman was based not so much on religion as on the law, which in all but a few states ignored her existence. In marrying she yielded to her husband both property and person, and the law would uphold him in demanding his "rights." If her children were starving, she could not work without his consent; and even then he could compel the employer to pay him her wages. Many a girl who brought her husband a handsome dowry spent the rest of her life on a beggarly allowance, all too literally called "pin money." But while a husband could call upon the courts to support him, he found it more convenient to appeal to his religion (which his wife was expected to embrace) as authority for the submission he claimed. Submission was the great female virtue. "Woman, noble and living satellite of man, follows through life in the orbit to which her husband draws her."[119] With the yet untempted Eve the pious wife was taught to say:

> My author and disposer, what thou bidd'st
> Unargued I obey. So God ordains:
> God is thy law, thou mine: to know no more
> Is woman's happiest knowledge, and her praise.[120]

But even though man was the divinely instituted head of the human family, wives were cautioned against expecting perfection. "We should all enter the marriage state," they were told, "remembering that we are about to be united to a fallen creature . . . from whom must be looked for much weakness and waywardness."[121] Stripped of its euphemism, the argument is briefly this: that chastity was less important in man than in woman; that a wife, without expostulating, should feign ignorance of her unfaithful husband's lapses and charm him back; that she should not expect the public to sympathize with a blazoning of her wrongs; and that to separate from her husband made her responsible for his later vices.[122] Even when his mind was inferior she was urged to be submissive:

I admit it is difficult for a sensible woman to submit to imbecility, but she should have considered this before she united herself to it. . . . One of the finest scenes, ever presented by the domestic economy, is that of a sensible woman employing her talents and address, not to subvert, but to support the authority of a weak husband. . . . The strength of woman lies not in resisting, but in yielding.[123]

There were violent protests against this doctrine. Mrs. Elizabeth Oakes Smith in an address on "The Sanctity of Marriage" declared that

in New-England, even, where it might be supposed that marriage might be less adulterated, it has become very much a household arrangement for thrift or economy, where a woman is selected for her domestic points, in the same manner that a housekeeper is secured.[124]

But such remarks were looked upon with disapproval, even by the fair housewives themselves, and dismissed as radicalism. Society kept up the polite fictions. Most husbands were faithful to their wives and provided for them. If the ardent love a girl dreamed of was never found, it was perhaps her own fault in expecting too much. "Gratitude is undoubtedly the foundation of the esteem we commonly feel for a husband,"[125] one lady confessed; and in public they all posed as sublimely happy.

It may have been perfunctory at times, but Mrs. Sigourney, years after love had fled, kept up a pretense of affection for her husband's "elegant and scientific mind." An honest admission that marriage vows could outlive the love they were founded in, besides being vulgar, would have deprived her of a most fruitful topic for moralizing. Except during brief visits to New Haven and Staten Island and a rather longer journey with friends to Niagara, she had sat opposite him at breakfast every morning for twenty-one years. She began to feel the need of a change. Mr. Sigourney was old at sixty-two, while she, thirteen years younger, was just approaching the pinnacle of literary fame, with a steady and increasing income. Her difficulty lay, not in writing poems, but in finding poems to write. Not without reason had Miss Edgeworth praised her skill in extracting verses from unlikely subjects. When there were no Pelicans on the Lake of Galilee[126] or African Mothers at Their Daughters' Graves,[127] she had been forced to look nearer home for her subjects. So humble a creature as the goose had provided a hundred lines of serious blank verse:

> I cannot bear to hear thee slander'd, Goose!
> It irketh me to see the truant boys
> Pause in their play, and cast a stone at thee,
> And call thee foolish.

Indeed, so generous is her spirit that she would

>   fain propose
> That, mid the poultry in the farmer's yard,
> The goose should wear a ducal coronet[128]

because his quill signs treaties of peace and reprieves for innocent prisoners. Another "poem" of equal length was

tortured from a bit of rag, whose imaginary history is
traced all the way from the cotton field, through manu-
facture and use, to its place on the housemaid's broom.
But that is just the introduction; there follow prophecies
of the rag's future forms in the pictured page

> Through which the lisping and delighted child
> Hath its first talk with knowledge, or the chart
> That saves the mariner mid rocks and shoals
> Upon the wrecking sea. . . .
> Or with some message from the Book of Life
> Wake[s] the dead slumber of benighted lands.[129]

But in spite of these lofty morals, occasional ill-natured
critics had spoken harshly of such subjects. Yes, she
needed a change.

Her parents, who had come to live in Hartford, had
both died. Mary, aged twelve, was beginning to disap-
point her mother by a callous attitude toward the things
"of immortal interest," engendered, perhaps, by the
hours she spent copying (in a "chirography" that would
bear scrutiny) long poems depicting heavenly joys; but
she could safely be left alone. Andrew was two years
younger, very diffident, and did not get on well with
other boys; but there was a boarding school where he
would be treated well for her sake. The Rev. John Williams, a professor at Washington College, was going
abroad with his mother; why shouldn't Mrs. Sigourney
join them?

Curiosity alone hardly seemed a sufficient motive to
take a mother from her two children; neither could she
explain that there was a scarcity of poetic raw material,
or that a few months' absence from her husband would
make life pleasanter for them all. But Dr. Brigham, the

family physician, who dispensed wholesome psychology with his potions, saw all her difficulties and suggested that a sea voyage was the very thing to clear up the lingering little cold that had troubled her for so long. Then her duty lay plain: she would tear herself from her loved ones, reluctantly and painfully, for her health's sake.

So she began at once collecting letters of introduction to all the celebrities in Great Britain. With some of them she had corresponded—that is, they had thanked her for the volume of poems she sent, or refused to contribute to the *Religious Souvenir*—and they were put on the list as acquaintances with whom no further formalities were necessary. Her publishers furnished other letters, including some to London booksellers; and Dwight, Mrs. Willard, and other friends who had traveled abroad gave her more. Those of the elect to whom none was forthcoming she put on a list to be considered after she had met the more accessible ones. Conspicuous among her boxes when she sailed August 1, 1840, was one full of her works, in various bindings suited to the rank of the great for whom they were destined.

The effect of the sea was exactly as Dr. Brigham had promised. The first day out Mrs. Sigourney's companions detected a faint flush of color in her cheeks, which increased day by day until the young college student in their group remarked that it was rather too bright to be natural. Her hair, too, took on a glossier hue; and the sea air, by a strange perversion of its customary action, caused certain little curls and ringlets not noticed before to peep from beneath her bonnet. A gay sprightliness of manner belying her fifty "summers" enlivened them all. Her pen had never sped so easily across the page or written more lines in an hour. Each day brought new sub-

jects: a land bird alighted on the boat a week out, and
died before their eyes; before evening she had a delicious
poem on the incident to read aloud in the cabin after
dinner, ending with the inevitable moral:

> Even thus, o'er life's unresting tide, . . .
> Ambition's votaries urge their way.[130]

And when they landed at Liverpool her journal held
enough new verses for a small volume, and plentiful ob-
servations in moralizing prose.

As a writer of travels, Mrs. Sigourney leaves much to
be desired. Like many Americans since, she was most impressed by the magnitude of the things she saw; her
notes are filled with the dimensions, extravagant costs,
and extreme antiquity of the monuments she visited.
"Our researches in the Bodleian and Radcliffe libraries,
the former of which contains 400,000 volumes, with
countless manuscripts, delighted us exceedingly," she
wrote.[131] Aesthetically she was without discrimination.
She felt an extraordinary reverence for the French taste
of the day. "From the saloon of the noble to the shop of
the petty marchand des modes," she says, "it is seen in
every variety of adornment, from the costly painting or
chiseled group of the ancient master, to the simple vase
of artificial flowers under its glass shade, or the little
fancy-clock, that hastens the movements of the needle."
The Louvre she mentions only as "that astonishing collection of 1500 arranged pictures, and probably as many
more for which the walls of its sumptuous gallery have no
space."[132]

The growing prudery of the age may explain her taste
in sculpture. Fifteen years before, a clerical friend from

Hartford visiting the Elgin Marbles had found them "not altogether proper for the indiscriminate admission of visitors of both sexes. . . . Indeed," he said, "it was not difficult to perceive, that the ladies here felt a little out of place."[133] In Paris, Mrs. Willard had found her favorite statues on the Pont Louis XVI; those in the Tuileries shocked her exceedingly with their nudity. "If your mothers were here," she wrote in a letter to her pupils at the Seminary, "I would leave you sitting on these shaded benches, and conduct them through the walks, and they would return, and bid you depart for our own America; where the eye of modesty is not publicly affronted; and where virgin delicacy can walk abroad without a blush." Of the Louvre she added: "I am not ashamed to say I have not visited the statuary. . . . I should rather be ashamed to say that I had."[134] Mrs. Sigourney, who had resolved to pick roses and not nettles, was less squeamish. She admired in the Louvre "a fine infant Mercury, and imagined among the effigies of the Emperors of Rome some resemblance to their real character, especially in the philosophic features of Marcus Aurelius, the thoughtful brow of Antoninus Pius, and the varied lineaments of Trajan, Severus, and Nerva, Domitian, Nero, and Caracalla." She found herself, however, most often attracted "towards a lovely, pensive Pol[y]hymnia" (her own sad Muse); and if she saw the Venus de Milo, she did not mention it.[135]

Her tour followed the regular itinerary of nineteenth-century travelers: from Liverpool to the Scottish lakes; Newcastle and York to London; two months in Paris; then back to London for three months of quiet adventure in the fringes of literary society. Wordsworth was the first lion she attacked. She had written to him some years before, soliciting poems for the *Religious Souvenir;* and when no reply came to her letter, she had appealed to R. Shelton Mackenzie, to whose annual, *The Forget-Me-Not,* she herself was a contributor, to find out if the poet had received it.

When I write to Wordsworth, in a few days [he assured her], I shall enquire if he got your letter. I think he did *not*—because, in his last, he wrote about you, and did not say you had written to him. I had a duplicate volume of the poems you sent me a copy of, and presented it to him—he speaks highly of such of its contents as his wife had read to him (his sight is bad & Mrs. W. acts as his amanuensis). The American Indians, in The Forget me Not he is delighted with. I hope—I almost think he will send me a short poem for you. Southey, another Sigourneyite, (if I may coin a word), I shall ask also, and by packet of March 16 [1838], all I get shall go to you.[136]

But neither of the great men had written for the *Religious Souvenir,* and the mystery of the unanswered letter was unexplained. It may have been a slight feeling of guilt in this matter that led Wordsworth to call so promptly at her inn when he learned Mrs. Sigourney was there and leave an invitation to tea at Rydal Mount. The whole family was assembled when she arrived, including Dorothy; to enter such a circle might well have awed a Hartford Poetess. But the simple surroundings and domestic conversation (the only literary phrase she could recall was one of the grandchildren's question whether *Ocean* were not the Christian name of the sea) soon put her at ease; and the impression of Wordsworth she wrote in her journal was the standard, sentimental one of the "sainted old man":

> . . . The evening lamp, that o'er thy silver locks
> And ample brow fell fitfully, and touched
> Thy lifted eye with earnestness of thought
> Are with me as a picture, ne'er to fade,
> Till death shall darken all material things.[137]

Her books had sold widely in Great Britain; one editor wrote her with pride that he alone had sold five thousand copies of *Letters to Young Ladies*.[138] In those days before international copyright, however, they had yielded her nothing but fame. So her first task on arriving in London was to arrange with the booksellers to publish three volumes for her. This done to her satisfaction, she saw the usual "sights" of the metropolis. But Westminster Abbey, the Tower, Mme Tussaud's, and Miss Linwood's embroidery show did not interest her nearly so much as the literary celebrities to whom she had notes of introduction.

The liveliest picture of these London visits is found in a letter of Mrs. Carlyle. For a decade all Americans of the slightest literary pretension had made pilgrimage to the little house in Cheyne Row. They did not always reach Carlyle; but "the Lion's Wife," as she called herself, was tormented with "applications from young ladies for autographs; passionate invitations to dine; announcements of inexpressible longings to drink tea" with the Carlyles, as well as a steady stream of visitors in the flesh.[139] "These Yankees form a considerable item in the ennuis of our mortal life," she wrote. "I counted lately fourteen of them in one fortnight, of whom Dr. Russel was the only one that you did not feel tempted to take the poker to."[140] One "ardent admirer," a young American beauty, whose clothes and complexion Mrs. Carlyle envied, she heard with her own ears "call out quite pas-

sionately at parting with him, 'Oh, Mr. Carlyle, I want
to see you to talk a long long time about—*Sartor*! . . .
What could such a young lady have got to say about *Sartor*, can you imagine?'' she asked indignantly.[141]

Mrs. Sigourney's letter of introduction, however,
found Carlyle in good spirits, and he replied at once:

> 5. CHEYNE ROW, CHELSEA,
> 3 Nov^r, 1840—
>
> MY DEAR MADAM,
> If you will do us the kindness to come to tea on Thursday
> Ev^g. at half past six, my wife will be happy to receive you;
> you will find us most probably alone; and we shall all hope to
> make a pleasant new acquaintance.
> Had I a Fortunatus' Hat, or even any swift wheel-vehicle, I
> should straightway seek out Denmark Hill, and deliver my message in person: but I hope you can dispense with that formality, in favour of a Pedestrian who is rather busy.
> > Believe me,
> > My dear Madam,
> > Yours very truly,
> > T. CARLYLE.[142]

But, as it happened, they were not alone on Thursday,
and Mrs. Carlyle, not at all happy to make a pleasant
new acquaintance, treated her very rudely. Whether or
not Mrs. Sigourney noticed this, she wrote politely to her
host, thanking him for the hospitality; and when Mrs.
Carlyle sent the note for Helen Welsh's autograph album, she described the way the evening was spent.

I send Helen an autograph of the American Poetess Mrs.
Sigourney—which does infinite credit to her total want of
penetration!—the evening of which she makes such grateful
mention—would have been remembered by anyone else with
feelings of quite another sort—even *I* who do not give much

way to remorse, have often had qualms of conscience in thinking about it. Her coming and still more her bringing along with
her two geerpoles of the name of "Johnson or Tomson," a male
and a female . . . her coming with this tag-ragery quite
spoiled a pleasant party that happened to be here—the Wedgwoods, Darwin, Mrs. Rich and Julia Smith—We had all set in
to be talkative and confidential—when this figure of an over-
the-water-Poetess—beplastered with rouge and pomatum—
bare-necked at an age which had left *certainty* far behind—
with long ringlets that never grew where they hung—smelling
marvellously of camphor or hartshorn and oil—all glistening in
black satin as if she were an apothecary's *puff* for black *stick-
ing-plaster*—and staring her eyes out, to give them animation
—stalked in and by the very barber-block-ish look of her reduced us all to silence—which effect was heightened by the pair
who followed at her heels—the *male* in an embroidered satin
vest—the *female* also in satin with—fancy it in *that* room—
and in *that* company!—with *a gold tiara on her head!* These
two never spoke a word but sat with their eyes fixed on Carlyle
as if they had paid their shillings at the door—Mrs. Sigourney
also made large eyes at him—and *she* took the liberty of pok-
ing at him now and then to make the lion roar, but he was not
in the vein—and would not roar finely that night for all she
could do. The rest of us meanwhile, feeling ourselves aggrieved
at being regarded with no more curiosity or politeness than as
many domestic cats in comparison of the Lion, repayed them
in their own coin—*I never addressed one word to them!* this is
a literal fact—of "her who helped to make that evening so
pleasant to remembrance." Faith it is not true that "we reap
not where we have not sown"—my harvests are far oftenest of
that highly improbable sort.[143]

Making liberal allowance for Mrs. Carlyle's headaches
and splenetic jealousy, as well as her aversion to Americans, there still remains a devastating authenticity in the
picture. The details are such as her rude silence would

Lydia H. Sigourney

From a Miniature by George Freeman, 1842. By Permission of The Wadsworth Atheneum.

have given her ample opportunity to observe. False hair, rouge, pomatum! Barenecked at fifty? In all charity let us hasten from Cheyne Row and its horrors and follow Mrs. Sigourney to Paris, where such matters pass unnoticed.

Of the usual sights there, Père La Chaise was her favorite; but the verses it inspired are far less stirring than those describing the greatest funeral she was ever to witness: "The Return of Napoleon from St. Helena."[144]

> Ho! City of the gay!
> Paris! what festal rite
> Doth call thy thronging million forth
> All eager for the sight?

It was not the first time Napoleon had appeared on her pages. Years before, when the second of Adoniram Judson's missionary wives had died at sea and been buried on St. Helena, Mrs. Sigourney wrote by request a piece called "The Two Graves"[145] that leaves little doubt of which sepulcher held, in her opinion, the worthier dust. Her thoughts reverted to this poem as she saw the Emperor's new tomb, surrounded by "a thousand trembling lamps"[146] and priests chanting continually "the pompous service of the Romish ritual."[147] The Seine was frozen over for the first time in years; driven by a gusty wind, little wreaths of snow went scudding along the black ice as she gazed across at the church towers, outposts of Popery, rising so menacingly above the city. Mrs. Judson lay forgotten on the rocky isle. But on the Day of Judgment even the French would be aware of her virtues. And undaunted by the tremendous emotion the funeral had evoked, Mrs. Sigourney added a stanza of protest against such adulation of the unrighteous Napoleon:

> Mysterious One, and proud!
>   In the land where shadows reign,
> Hast thou met the flocking ghosts of those,
>   Who at thy nod were slain?
> Oh, when the cry of that spectral host,
>   Like a rushing blast shall be,
> What will thine answer be to them?
> And what thy God's to thee?[148]

These ominous queries were addressed to the *Soldier* rather than the *Emperor*. For royalty Mrs. Sigourney shared the same predilection that prompted all the other Americans abroad to be presented at court. Louis Philippe at the moment was showing the world how monarchy and democracy could be combined in one person; and his affability, particularly toward Americans, was famous. Patriotic citizens from the new world, whose fathers had fought under Washington, crowded in to gaze at the sovereign and to see at first hand the ostentatious magnificence of his court. The ladies found it a good excuse for a new dress; and their husbands, in hired regimentals, clutching awkwardly the laced chapeaux and dangling swords, escorted them bravely to the Tuileries, where forty or fifty Americans were sometimes presented in one evening. Ranged under the protecting wing of the American Minister, Lewis Cass, they stared wide-eyed at "the elite of many lands" until the murmur of "The King! the King!" warned them of the monarch's approach. When it came her turn, Mrs. Sigourney was introduced as a New England poetess. The following momentous conversation ensued:

"In what part of New England do you reside?" the king inquired. "In Connecticut." "Ah! I have been in Connecticut. It has a fine river. And I have been in Norwich, and New London, and New Haven. They are all pleasant places." Passing on a step or two, he turned and said, "And I have been in Hartford too. That also is a pleasant place."[149]

And with this impartial bestowal of compliment, so typical of his career, he disappeared down the line. The absence of any term of address such as ''Your Majesty'' and the fact that in later editions various alterations are made in the King's words might lead one to suspect the accuracy of the report. The whole incident sounds better in the poetical version written the next day:[150]

'T was sweet to hear,
In the bright throne-room of the Tuileries,
And from the lip of Europe's wisest king,
The name of my own river, and the spot
Where I was born, coupled with kindly words,
As one tenacious of their scenery,
Through many a lustrum.

The Queen, praised as the pattern of conjugal virtues, came next, walking down the line behind the King, instead of standing to await the presentations; after her came the royal princes and princesses in great array, greeting the Americans in English with every semblance of pleasure. The whole atmosphere was so unlike the haughty reception she expected that Mrs. Sigourney could not contain her surprise.

We found
More of simplicity than we had deemed
Abode in courts; and this to us, who love
Our plain republic, was a circumstance
Not to be overlooked.

A reader might fairly expect such verses to end without a moral; but even the French court struck the didactic note. After discussing the Queen's domestic affairs,
Mrs. Sigourney adds:

> And I was pleased to see
> She had the queenly grace of prudence too,
> In lesser things; and on this wintry night
> Drew downward to the wrist the lengthened sleeve,
> And bade her satin robe protect the chest,
> Deeming most justly, that vitality
> And health outweighed the tinsel modes of dress,
> Coined by the milliner.

That would answer Mary the next time she asked to have
her new dress made with short sleeves. But it was a trifle
compared with the more intimate bit that followed:

> I have heard
> From good authority, and am right glad
> To tell it here, that many a leading belle
> Of fashion and nobility in France
> Abjure the corset, and maintain a form
> Erect and graceful, without busk or cord,
> Ambitious to bequeath a name, unstained
> By suicide. Would that my friends at home,
> Those sweet young blossoms on my country's stem,
> Might credit the report, and give their lungs
> And heart fair play, and earn a hope to reach
> The dignity of threescore years and ten,
> Free from the taint of self-derived disease.

A beautifully bound volume of poems transmitted
with a letter through Mr. Cass brought from the Queen a
curt acknowledgment in the hand of a lady-in-waiting. It
was soon followed by a diamond bracelet. This gift, as a

mark of royal favor, proved to be an excellent advertisement. Biographical notices henceforth frequently mentioned that the "Empress of the French" had bestowed it upon Mrs. Sigourney after reading her poems, although good Queen Amélie could scarcely understand English. Popular legend expanded the details and related how the Queen had taken the bracelet from her wrist and given it to Mrs. Sigourney with her own hand; later, people to whom one queen was as good as another, transferred the whole episode to the Court of St. James's and made Victoria the donor. But the youthful Victoria, though she may have been favored with a presentation volume, was never officially aware of Mrs. Sigourney's presence in London.

The letters of introduction now went broadcast. London was used to visiting Americans, and for the most part accepted them cheerfully, if somewhat condescendingly. Calling one morning at Joanna Baillie's, Mrs. Sigourney met Samuel Rogers. She had admired and imitated his poetry from her girlhood, having quoted the last ten lines of *Pleasures of Memory* in *Moral Pieces*[151] in 1815. And now the suave kindliness of this incredible octogenarian, who combined all the qualities of the "sainted old man" with the gay flattery of youth, quite fascinated her. At his invitation she went to see his treasures and curiosities, including Milton's receipt for *Paradise Lost,* and poured out to him the story of her dear children. Another day Mrs. Fry, the philanthropic Quakeress, showed her through Newgate, describing the work she had done among the female prisoners. And Mrs. Sigourney called at her house and told, in turn, of her own work in the Connecticut State Prison, and sent some volumes of poems to be distributed among the unfortunate women.[152]

But in spite of the excitement of meeting famous people and inhaling the incense of flattery, she was very homesick. She had been abroad less than six months; it seemed like years. In January when she went to see Queen Victoria open Parliament, she amused herself "with finding, or fancying, likenesses between the distinguished personages, and friends at home."[153] And whenever she met a slender boy dressed in the brown-linen apron and black belt that Andrew sometimes wore, everything else faded from her sight. "It mattered not, that a spot hallowed by history, an ancient castle, or a solemn cathedral, which from childhood she had been anxious to behold, were pointed out to her."[154] She was entirely absorbed in wondering how little Andrew fared among rough boys who did not understand his sensitive nature; and the sad, violet eyes stared at her reproachfully, dim through the April mists. At such moments no one offered her more comfort than Mrs. Jameson. A warm friendship sprang up between them; and the day before she sailed for New York, she received this effusive letter:

MY DEAR DEAR MRS. SIGOURNEY—
Though I am coming round myself with the hope of being able to render some little assistance in your preparations yet I cannot let my little maid pass without sending you a line to thank you for the dear little book you so kindly sent me . . . I shall prize this last volume as the parting gift of one whom we have so highly esteemed so deeply loved. Would that we could keep you amongst us! . . .
             Believe me
                My dear dear friend
                    Your sincerely & gratefully
                      attached friend
                      MARY ANN JAMESON[155]

A few moments of sentimental reverie were spent at Barley Wood, where in 1815 Miss Hannah More had received Miss Huntley's *Moral Pieces* from the hand of Mr. Gallaudet; and the next day Mrs. Sigourney had her last glimpse of England from the smoky deck of the *Great Western*. Off the Grand Bank the ship ran into a great ice field. Evening worship was just over when the first berg appeared; soon they were surrounded by them. To the mind of a poetess it seemed a cosmic drama, which heavenly bodies were watching as anxiously as the Deity himself.

On this strange and appalling scene the stars looked out, one after another, with their calm, pure eyes. All at once a glare of splendor burst forth, and a magnificent aurora borealis went streaming up the concave. . . . And there they were, dashing and drifting around us, those terrible kings of the Arctic, in their mountain majesty, while, like the tribes in the desert, our mysterious path was between the pillar of cloud, and the pillar of flame.[156]

The boat headed south, still surrounded by the field ice. During the night Dr. Wayland, President of Brown University, stayed in his stateroom and prayed; Mrs. Sigourney planned verses. And "by nine in the morning," she recorded piously, ". . . it pleased God to set us free from this great danger."[157]

Maria Edgeworth read the poetical description of this night with mild amusement.

Thank you [she wrote Mrs. Sigourney] for your interesting account of the icebergs.—Quite sublime—when one is in danger it is a great comfort to think that it is a sublime danger one that will tell well afterwards and that will be a thing to talk over the fireside to the latest hour of ones life—to ones great nephews & nieces on St Crispins Eve—[158]

Their acquaintance had begun in 1836 when Miss Edgeworth wrote some overgenerous comments on *Select Poems,* which Mrs. Sigourney had sent her. She had been a little annoyed to find extracts from this letter published in the later editions of the book; and it was with some anxiety, therefore, that she wrote on Mrs. Sigourney's return to America:

> Much wiser not to publish at least immediately after a visit to foreign country—Better leave the impressions first to cool and consolidate by time & the facts to be verified & generalized by further experience.
>
> And now that I have written this perhaps I should not have written it to you.—I hope you will not be hurt or offended if you really are writing anything about your visit to England. But I hope still more and honestly I tell it to you that you are not.[159]

Mrs. Sigourney *was.* Before she had set out on her travels she had planned to write about them. Her conscience was not altogether clear as to how much she ought to respect the venerable Miss Edgeworth's counsel; and she laid her doubts before her friend Alexander Everett, then President of Jefferson College, Louisiana.

> Let me entreat you [he replied] not to be dissuaded from publishing your travels by the letter,—I had almost said the *twaddle,*—of Miss Edgeworth, of which you have sent me an extract. . . . If your fair counsellor had acted on her own advice to you, she would never have published a line. If you had acted on it heretofore, you would never have written a verse.
>
> As to "waiting for first impressions to cool," Miss E. seems to have forgotten, that the warmth, belonging to first impressions, is precisely the living principle of a book of travels. . . . If you have notes and materials in hand, my dear Mrs.

Sigourney, let me earnestly advise you to publish them immediately. Trust implicitly, without fear of criticism, to your own good sense and good taste as to what you ought to make known. Your own instinctive sympathies with the Beautiful & Good will be a sure guide as to the opinion of the public.[160]

The notes and materials Mrs. Sigourney had, consisted of a journal in verse and prose, kept carefully during the whole time she was away, and every communication, no matter how trivial, she had received from famous persons abroad. She even preserved the brief note Byron's sister wrote Mrs. Hall, refusing to ask Mrs. Sigourney to an "at home."[161] The assiduity with which these shadows of acquaintance were nursed into "literary friendships" is pathetically revealed in her correspondence. Joanna Baillie, for example, who was depicted quite intimately in the journal, expressed a mild surprise "that you have kept me so kindly in your remembrance after such a short—almost momentary acquaintance."[162] Samuel Rogers, sending a copy of his *Italy* in return for her books, expressed the same idea more flatteringly:

MY DEAR MRS SIGOURNEY
Your first letter welcomed me on my return from Paris, where I had idled away a month or two, & I was in the very act of thanking you for it when the second arrived. Alas, how much I regret that your visit to my house was so short, & that when you left my door, you were never again to cross the threshold. Not that I despair, when you may come in a fortnight; & pray, pray, when you do so, bring Her who reads to you in your winter evenings [i.e. Mary], along with you. Pray give my love to Her & tell her that, old as I am, my heart is as young as ever & my eyes are as ready to glisten & overflow at the kindness that I should experience at such a meeting. May God bless her,

& may she live to be a blessing to you & to others—long after
I am gone & forgotten!

Your much obliged
& very sincere friend
S. Rogers

St. James's Place
Augst 22, 1842 . . .[163]

With the Countess of Blessington, Mrs. Sigourney
maintained a correspondence for several years, but it
was never of a confidential nature. Mrs. Hall had taken
her to call at Gore House, and shortly after her return to
Hartford, Mrs. Sigourney wrote:

Your Ladyship's writings . . . are known in this country.
Still, I should like to have them more so, for the Young, Green
West is inclined to appreciate genius and taste. Might I ask,
that if you condescend to reply to this, you will send me at the
same time a few lines of your poetry?[164]

Lady Blessington complied more graciously than her
gushing correspondent had expected, inclosing a "sweet
poem."

The very sweetness of its nature [Mrs. Sigourney wrote] has
frustrated my hopes. I had desired to adorn a periodical cir-
culated very widely among American ladies, with some original
effusion of yours, but the very flattering manner in which it al-
ludes to me, and which would be considered on this side of the
water as exceedingly beyond my deserts, will oblige me to con-
fine the tuneful guest to my own portfolio.[165]

Mrs. Sigourney next sent a present of her books:

I have perused your poems [the Countess purled in reply]
with a pleasure such as one feels when wandering amid a beautiful parterre of rich and fragrant flowers, each, and all, at-

tracting new admiration. How well your American publishers bring out (as the craft term it) your books.[166]

And sending in turn a small book and some "new fashioned material for a dress," she asked for a picture of Mrs. Sigourney. There was none that her "friends" were satisfied with, Mrs. Sigourney responded, but she would send a copy of one that was under way from a portrait made in London.

I recollect your requesting of me [she continued], when in England, a lock of hair, which was forgotten to be sent while I was there. Will you now allow it to cross the ocean in the form of a simple bracelet, accompanied by a bottle of the pure otto of rose, which I have recently received from Constantinople?

Mary, for whom Stamatiades had really intended a half interest in the perfume, suffered further in this aristocratic levy and sent the niece of the Countess a little purse, "the work of the poor aborigines of the country."[167] After about two years the intervals between letters grew longer and the presents dwindled to little writing boxes or note paper, until, finally, the correspondence ended, as it had begun, with a letter from America.

Among the introductions Mrs. Sigourney took with her to Europe there was one to Robert Southey; but Wordsworth had told her at Rydal Mount of the Laureate's insanity and advised her not to go to Keswick. She eased her disappointment in a sort of sonnet written the same day, and sent it off to Mrs. Southey, the former Caroline Bowles.

> I thought to see thee in thy lake-girt home,
>   Thou of creative soul! I thought with thee
> Amid thy mountain solitudes to roam,
>   And hear the voice, whose echoes wild and free

Had strangely thrilled me, when my life was new,
  With old romantic tales of wondrous lore;
But ah! they told me that thy mind withdrew
  Into its mystic cell,—nor evermore

Sate on the lip, in fond, familiar word,
  Nor through the speaking eye *her* love repaid,
Whose heart for thee with ceaseless care is stirred,
  Both night and day; upon the willow shade

Her sweet harp hung. They told me, and I wept,
  As on my pilgrim way o'er England's vales I kept.[168]

Mrs. Southey, herself a poetess, could not resist the sympathetic inquiries of her sister singer, and she replied with a fulness of detail she was later to regret. For when *Pleasant Memories of Pleasant Lands* appeared in December, 1842, she was amazed to find, following a quotation from her poem *The Pauper's Death-Bed,* this extraordinary information:

In this exquisite picture may we not see the germ of the same tenderness, which watches night and day in the darkened cell, where a glorious mind has withdrawn from its former intercourse with the living? I trust to be forgiven for selecting from one of her recent letters, a few passages for the friends, who in this western world have admired, in almost every department of literature, the inventive genius of Dr. Southey, his comprehensive learning, and his astonishing industry.

"You desire to be remembered to him who sang, 'of Thalaba, the wild, and wondrous tale.' Alas, my friend, the dull cold ear of death is not more insensible than his, my dearest husband's, to all communication from the world without. Scarcely can I keep hold of the last poor comfort of believing that he still knows me. This almost complete unconsciousness has not been of more than six months' standing, though more than two years have elapsed, since he has written even his name. After the death of his first wife, the 'Edith' of his first love, who was for several years insane, his health was terribly shaken. Yet for the greater part of a year that he spent with me, in Hampshire, my former home, it seemed perfectly reëstablished, and he used to say, 'It had surely pleased God, that the last years of his life should be happy.' But the Almighty will was otherwise. The little cloud soon appeared, which was in no long time to overshadow all. In the blackness of its shadow we still live, and shall pass from under it only through the portals of the grave.

"The last three years have done on me the work of twenty. The one, sole business of my life is that, which I verily believe keeps the life in me, the guardianship of my dear, helpless, unconscious husband."[169]

Quotations from this chapter appeared in the English papers in February; but it was not until after Southey's death in March that the storm broke over Mrs. Sigourney. *The Story Teller* published an account of the affair (which the editor later insisted rested on the authority of Mrs. Southey's own handwriting) pointing out that Mrs. Sigourney was a complete stranger, never having seen Mrs. Southey, and declaring that this letter, the only one she had received, was "interpolated with phrases implying intimacy and ejaculations of pathos," none of which Mrs. Southey had ever penned. When a friend of Mrs. Sigourney attacked the *London Athenaeum* for reprinting the story, the editor pointed out "Alas, my friend" as both an ejaculation of pathos and a phrase implying intimacy, and continued:

But this is a minor point, and we are quite content to leave it in abeyance. The real question is the moral wrong in publishing a private letter at all, especially such a letter so obtained—a letter . . . so "painful and affecting" that we noticed it with reluctance—a letter which we described as too "sad and sacred" for the common gaze—a letter so solemn in its revelation that,

in our charity, we assumed that it could only have become public by strange inadvertence or accident—but which we now
learn was published by this "high-principled lady" herself, as
soon after her return to America as she could hurry a volume
through the press.[170]

In America, Mrs. Sigourney's friends came at once to
her rescue. Mr. Wadsworth and another prominent gentleman wrote a letter for the Hartford *Courant*, absolv-
ing her from the charge of interpolation. That of publishing private letters without authority, however, rested
heavy upon her, in spite of the blatantly patriotic efforts
of a friend [Ann Stephens?] in *The Brother Jonathan*,
who regarded the unfortunate quotation as "nothing
more or less than a bulletin of Southey's health and a
matter of public interest, [which] could by no means be
distorted into a breach of confidence."[171] Out of "some
millions" of persons who know Mrs. Sigourney through
her writings and love her for her worth, only one in ten
thousand, the article continued, has the vaguest notion
of who Mrs. Southey is, and that is principally through
her connection with the laureate. "That Mrs. Sigourney
requires the countenance of any woman in England, even
the Queen herself, to lift her one degree in the estimation
of us Yankees—is exquisitely farcial." But such remarks and the milder protests of Mrs. Hall[172] in London
did not disperse the clouds of suspicion that hung thick
over the affair. A report that Mrs. Southey had written
cordially to Mrs. Sigourney, exculpating her, was certainly unfounded. And in July, still troubled, she wrote
Professor Silliman:

It has recently been suggested to me, that if some person of
high standing in society, and whose name, like yours, had
weight on the other side of the Atlantic would certify to the

authenticity of the few sentences taken from Mrs. Southey's letter, the grave charge of interpolation, which rests rather heavily upon a moral writer, might be removed.[173]

It is probable that in the troubled days of her husband's illness, Mrs. Southey wrote with more warmth than she remembered; yet one must sympathize a little with the bewildered English editor who declared that "there has been a great deal of duplicity."[174]

Mrs. Southey was not the only one who had cause to complain of *Pleasant Memories,* for it also contained extracts from letters of Miss Edgeworth, Miss Mitford, and Mrs. Hall. Mrs. Hall apparently did not object to the advertising; but Miss Mitford, like Mrs. Southey, had never seen Mrs. Sigourney, though the way she is mentioned in the book would lead every reader to think them old friends.[175] The letter quoted referred to her father, an extravagant good-for-nothing, whom she had given her whole life to nursing, and who had died about the same time as Southey. But she was a gentle and amiable person, and wrote Mrs. Sigourney to thank her for the "beautiful volume which has given great pleasure in England. It is full of beauty & of interest . . . the only doubtful point being the publishing of private letters however kindly intended. I do not so much mean my own as Mrs Southey's. . . ."[176]

Maria Edgeworth, who had suffered before in having her letter used as a puff for *Select Poems,* was more specific.

Your very candid and touching letter made the impression upon me which you desired—and I completely acquit you of any unworthy motives—I know nothing about the affair you mention of Mrs Southey's letters except what the newspaper and you have told me—and I am glad to have the newspaper statements set right by yours—to which I give credit without requiring to see the original letter which you from honorable motives withhold.

As to my own letters & whatever praise I gave to your works I can only repeat what I said before that I am sure whatever I said was perfectly sincere—and I should rejoice if my name or my opinion could be of any use to you—I only request that my *letters* should not be published—You are quite at liberty to shew whatever I said, or say, to any friends you may wish to shew it to—

And if you like, and think it worthwhile so to do, publish in any newspaper or journal you please the following

"Miss Edgeworth has expressed high approbation of the "poems of Mrs Sigourney*—She admires both the poetical "genius and the moral sentiments of this American writer— "and we have reason to believe that Miss E was much pleased "by Mrs Sigourney's unaffected, unpresuming manners, and by "her conversation when she saw her in London during her visit "there"

This I write *for publication* as a paragraph *not a letter* I hope it may meet your wishes.[177]

It would seem impossible to misunderstand this attitude; but Mrs. Sigourney wrote once again, asking in particular about the quotation. This time Miss Edgeworth reiterated her ideas more forcibly.

I should not like to have any *letter* or *extract* from any letter of mine published but you may put the opinions in the form you copied for me in the *paragraph* as you call it from the letter of Sep 4th 43 beginning with

Miss E has expressed high approbation of the poems of Mrs Sigourney &c

I do *not* like to have the *extract* from the letter of Sep 15th

---

* Miss Edgeworth first wrote ''has expressed *to Mrs Sigourney her admiration of her volume of poems.*''

36—published in that form—I do not like that the sentiments should be quoted in the first person thus

"*I* particularly admire" &c. . . . .

I cannot let them be *quoted* from my letter or appear as from a letter of mine.—

And as to writing any new letter or *notice* of your poem Pocahanta—or Pleasant Memories—Excuse me, but I really could not do this bespoken for publication—It would be quite foreign to my habits and assuredly if I could bring myself to do it I should not do it naturally or well and it would lower the value of my sincere praise given from my heart spontaneously —and would injure me with the public without serving you—

I hope my dear M^rs. S I shall not either hurt or offend you by this plain speaking—No—you will feel that you may depend upon the perfect sincerety of my approbation and of all the feelings which I *have* expressed for your writings and your character.[178]

Their correspondence was not interrupted by these flurries; little gifts still found their way to Ireland—Indian slippers represented as "the work of the Princess of one of the aboriginal tribes," slips of rose bushes, and packets of convolvulus seeds from Mary; and the long letters in reply are filled with exciting accounts of the murder of landlords and the threatened potato failure.[179] Yet with all her cordiality, Miss Edgeworth never again wrote anything that Mrs. Sigourney would be tempted to use for advertising. The unauthorized letter of praise disappeared for a time from *Select Poems;* but, after Miss Edgeworth's death in 1849, it was restored, not, of course, as a letter, but as "extracts from a communication of the late lamented Maria Edgeworth." The impersonal tone was maintained until that last, glowing compliment; there the forbidden pronoun (*me,* not *I*) crept back:

Another remark has occurred to me in reading these poems, that Mrs. Sigourney appears to have the power of writing *extempore* on passing subjects, and at the moment they are called for.[180]

Mrs. Southey's letter, similarly, was omitted from the second edition of *Pleasant Memories*. When a third edition was called for in 1856 Mrs. Sigourney had no intention of reprinting the two pages of gushing tribute to the laureate's second wife. Mrs. Southey had been two years in her grave, else she might have been amused to see herself referred to as ''the successor of his beloved Edith.''

CHAPTER FOUR

THE AMERICAN HEMANS

IN 1828 Mrs. Sigourney shared with N. P. Willis a prize of $100 offered by *The Token,* the first successful American annual.[181] The prominence the prize gave her made her name indispensable to the "gemmy" little volumes that began to appear in shoals; and she rode to fame in the thirties on a swelling wave of gilt-edged, silk-bound annuals. In the forties, when the wave broke, she had already transferred her attention to the magazines, on whose voluminous tide her reputation, buoyed up by a vast deal of foam, was supported until her death. Professional moralists inveighed against the magazines and set forth in elaborate rhetoric the evils they wrought on young minds. Many thoughtful people, Mr. Sigourney among them, deplored the great increase of periodicals. But everyone else subscribed to them and read them. "The whole tendency of the age," wrote Poe, "is Magazine-ward."[182]

Professor Beers has pointed out the ease with which a "national reputation" was to be attained in those days.[183] If one caught the fancy of a few hundreds of readers in New York, Philadelphia, and Boston, and secured the praise of some dozens of journals, he was acclaimed at once a "national poet." Logrolling and mutual admiration were notorious, powerful, and feared. Extravagant puffs copied from paper to paper could make an author famous; maliciously unfair strictures could as quickly damn him, without regard to the merit of his writings. In this circle of reputation-mongers it was the fashion to compare native writers with the English authors they most resembled, and rarely to the detriment of the Americans. Thus, Cooper was labeled "the American Scott,"[184] and Mrs. Sigourney, by the same token, became "the American Hemans."[185] An editorial accident, in her case, had strengthened the comparison: In 1828 a New Haven printer, publishing an edition of Mrs. Hemans' poetical works, added by mistake a poem of Mrs. Sigourney's called *Death of an Infant:*

> Death found strange beauty on that cherub brow,
> And dash'd it out.—There was a tint of rose
> On cheek and lip,—he touched the veins with ice,
> And the rose faded;—forth from those blue eyes
>
> There spake a wishful tenderness,—a doubt
> Whether to grieve or sleep, which Innocence
> Alone can wear. With ruthless haste he bound
> The silken fringes of their curtaining lids
>
> For ever;—there had been a murmuring sound,
> With which the babe would claim its mother's ear,
> Charming her even to tears. The spoiler set
> His seal of silence.—But there beamed a smile
>
> So fixed and holy from that marble brow,—
> Death gazed, and left it there;—he dared not steal
> The signet-ring of Heaven.[186]

Mrs. Sigourney's "friends"—those convenient anonymous persons who always made the protests that modesty forbade her—soon informed the public that the poem was not by Mrs. Hemans, but by Mrs. Sigourney, and might be found in the 1827 volume of *Poems*. Naturally, the fair author was pleased by the incident; for many years she wrote *Death of an Infant,* with several felicitous changes, in young ladies' albums. And the reviewers were soon echoing "the American Hemans" back and forth whenever there was occasion to mention Mrs. Sigourney.

But in 1835 there was one omnivorous reader of poetry who was angered by the comparison, a young man named Poe, whose brilliant criticism—almost the only genuine American criticism of the first half of the century—was spreading his fame with that of the *Southern Literary Messenger.* Poe had a mania for finding resemblances, even where they did not exist; and to him such phrases as "the American Hemans" were tantamount to an accusation of plagiarism. He had an undisguised contempt for the shameless puffing by which the literary *Epizæ,* as he called them, succeeded "in creating for themselves an absolutely positive reputation, by mere dint of the continuity and perpetuity of their appeals to the public."

We cannot, then, regard the microscopical works of the *animalculæ* in question, as simple nothings [he wrote in *Marginalia*]; for they produce, as I say, a positive effect, and no multiplication of zeros will result in unity—but as negative quantities—as less than nothings; since — into — will give +.[187]

Reviewing Mrs. Sigourney's *Zinzendorff and Other Poems* in the *Messenger* for January, 1836, he expressed himself on both points:

Mrs. Sigourney has long been known as an author. Her earliest publication was reviewed about twenty years ago in the North American. . . . The fame which she has since acquired is extensive; and we, who so much admire her virtues and her talents, and who have so frequently expressed our admiration of both in this Journal—we, of all persons—are the least inclined to call in question the justice or accuracy of the public opinion, by which has been adjudged to her so high a station among the *literati* of our land. Some things, however, we cannot pass over in silence. There are two kinds of popular reputation,—or rather there are two roads by which such reputation may be attained. . . . Let us suppose two writers having a reputation apparently equal—that is to say, their names *being equally in the mouths of the people.* . . . The one has written a great work. . . . And let us imagine that, by this single effort, the author has attained a certain quantum of reputation. We know it to be possible that another writer of very moderate powers may build up for himself, little by little, a reputation equally great—and, this too, merely by keeping continually in the eye, or by appealing continually with little things, to the ear, of that great, overgrown, and majestical gander, the critical and bibliographical rabble.

It would be an easy, although perhaps a somewhat disagreeable task, to point out several of the most popular writers in America—popular in the above mentioned sense—who have manufactured for themselves a celebrity by the very questionable manner, to which we have alluded. But it must not be thought that we wish to include Mrs. Sigourney in the number. By no means. She has trod, however, upon the confines of their circle. She does not *owe* her reputation to the chicanery we mention, but it cannot be denied that it has been thereby greatly assisted. In a word—no single piece which she has written, and not even her collected works as we behold them in the present volume, and in the one published some years ago, would fairly entitle her to that exalted rank which she actually enjoys as the authoress, *time after time,* of her numerous, and, in most instances, very creditable compositions. The validity of our objections to this adventitious notoriety we must be allowed to consider unshaken, until it can be proved that any multiplication of zeros will eventuate in the production of a unit.

We have watched, too, with a species of anxiety and vexation brought about altogether by the sincere interest we take in Mrs. Sigourney, the progressive steps by which she has at length acquired the title of the "American Hemans." Mrs. S. cannot conceal from her own discernment that she has acquired this title *solely by imitation.* The very phrase "American Hemans" speaks loudly in accusation: and we are grieved that what by the over-zealous has been intended as complimentary should fall with so ill-omened a sound into the ear of the judicious. We will briefly point out those particulars in which Mrs. Sigourney stands palpably convicted of that sin which in poetry is not to be forgiven. . . .

Poe then details the evidence: her subjects are like Mrs. Hemans'; both use similar types of verse; both indulge in apostrophe, and too frequent interjections such as *yea!* and *alas!* But his principal objection is that the long mottoes and quotations the ladies set for their texts destroy "what is rightly termed by Schlegel, 'the *unity or totality of interest.*' " This was a favorite idea of Poe's; and the paragraph discussing it reappears almost word for word in the famous review of Longfellow's *Ballads.*

Having expressed ourselves thus far in terms of nearly unmitigated censure, it may appear in us as somewhat equivocal to say that, as Americans, we are proud—very proud of the talents of Mrs. Sigourney. Yet such is the fact. The faults which we have already pointed out, and some others which we will point out hereafter, are but dust in the balance, when weighed against her very many and distinguishing excellences. Among those high qualities which give her, beyond doubt, a title to the sacred name of poet are an acute sensibility to natural loveliness—a quick and perfectly just conception of the

moral and physical sublime—a calm and unostentatious vigor
of thought—a mingled delicacy and strength of expression—
and above all, a mind nobly and exquisitely attuned to all the
gentle charities and lofty pieties of life.

There is a concrete quality in his statement of the
faults of her verse that is much more convincing than
such tenuous excellences as "a quick and perfectly just
conception of the moral and physical sublime"; and
when one finishes the review with its catalogue of alternate good and bad passages, he rather suspects Poe of
irony in declaring that the following lines find a ready
echo in his bosom:

> Oh, speak no ill of Poetry,
> For 't is a holy thing!

What did he really think? A half-serious note in *Marginalia* says: "Where the gentler sex is concerned, there
seems but one course for the critic—speak if you can
commend—be silent, if not. . . ."[188] Just how far Poe
followed his dictum one cannot tell; the mixture of
kindliness and severity with which he always mentions
Mrs. Sigourney makes it difficult to determine his real
opinion. Yet in answering charges of "slashing" brought
against the *Messenger* he listed the review of *Zinzendorff*
among those in which "praise slightly prevails."[189] And
if he had considered it oversevere, he would hardly have
sent a copy to the fair victim herself.

The first reading of the article to which his charming
letter called her attention convinced Mrs. Sigourney that
Poe was not a person she could combat on questions of
criticism. He was much too dangerous to have for an
enemy. So she replied to his letter with a simplicity and

candor that few of her female contemporaries could have achieved :

HARTFORD, CONN\ᵀ., April 23ᵈ 1836.

MY DEAR SIR,—

Please to accept my thanks for your letter of the 12th with the January number of the "Southern Literary Messenger," which I had not before seen. I am happy to discover the present Editor of my favourite periodical, and also to perceive how much it profits by the guidance of that powerful pen, whose versatile and brilliant creations, I have often admired.

With regard to the article which has elicited our correspondence, allow me to premise, that few entertain more exalted opinions of the majesty of criticism than myself, and of its salutary influence on national literature, when independently, yet candidly exercised. I have felt that the living writers of our country, especially those of my own sex, had been too indiscriminately fed on praise. At least, in my own case, the courtesy of the publick has so far transcended my deserts, that were it not for the deep consciousness of imperfection, I should scarcely have retained hope of improvement. With these sentiments, I should not probably be over sensitive on the subject of a review, or be restive under discipline, which I had sought to establish.—

At the same time I confess that there are points in yours, for which I was not perfectly prepared.—The exposition, however severe, of any faults in style, spirit, or construction, which I might have reformed,—would have been held cause of gratitude. But the character of a determined imitator,—and one whose reputation has been greatly assisted by chicanery,— seem to impeach both intellectual and moral integrity.—If founded in justice, they truly demand a "purgation with euphrasy and rue." . . . I would not for a moment admit the idea that there is ought of equality between my writings, and that of the most gifted poet of the age, so recently reclaimed to her native sphere. [Mrs. Hemans]—The resemblance, which my friends have imagined to exist, I have resolved into their partiality. The contents of a volume of poems, published in 1814 & selected by a friend from journals, written in early youth, without a thought of publication, & another in 1821, [*Traits of the Aborigines*] were composed before I had heard of Mrs. Hemans, and likewise one of 1827,—most of whose poems were in existence, before I had enjoyed the pleasure of perusing any of hers,—can therefore not be classed as imitations of that pure model.

But that I have now transgressed a rule long since adopted, not to remark on any unfavorable criticism,—must be imputed to the courtesy of your letter,—which surely merited a friendly reply, and with sincere wishes for the success of the work under your auspices,—and a benedicite on Virginia, which I love,— I remain yours,

with high respect & esteem,

L. H. SIGOURNEY[190]

At this point the correspondence rested some weeks. Then, when Poe was planning a special number of the *Messenger* that was to consist "entirely of articles from our most distinguished *literati*," he wrote Mrs. Sigourney a tactful letter, saying that he feared the review had so offended her that she would not deign to contribute. With the utmost frankness she replied:

HARTFORD, June 11th, 1836.

MY DEAR SIR,—

Yours of the 4th was this morning received, and I hasten to assure you that your apprehension of having forfeited my good-will, is entirely groundless.—It is surely a hard case, if a critic may not express his opinions, freely, and even severely, in this land of freedom. All that an author can expect, in such a case, is to explain, if he supposes there has been ought of misconception. This I ventured to do.—But to cherish vindic-

tiveness, is quite another affair, & I assure you, forms no part
of my creed. There is surely, enough of controversy abroad in
our land, without its few literati lifting up the tomahawk, and
scalping-knife against each other. . . .

—I send at your request, what I happen to have by me,—
and as you will have it to be a peace offering, you can thus
view it, though there is in reality, no truce to be made between
us. Do not, however, assume a more lenient style with regard to
me, in consequence of any little aid I may have afforded the
"Messenger," since no traffick in civilities is as valuable in my
opinion as sincerity. Yours, with respect, and in

perfect good temper,
L. H. Sigourney . . .[191]

The poem she sent, a biblical one called *The Ruler's
Faith,* held the place of honor in the August number;
tucked obscurely in the middle of the magazine was Poe's
Israfel.

The charge of imitating Mrs. Hemans can be dismissed
quickly. There are no passages in Mrs. Sigourney's
poems that one can say were *plagiarized* from her. To be
sure, if there were any, Poe would have discovered them,
for he had an extraordinary ear for detecting echoes. It
is more accurate to say, perhaps, that Mrs. Sigourney
modeled her verse on that of others. In the earlier works
the model was Hannah More, or Rogers, or Cowper; later
it was Coleridge, or Wordsworth, or Byron. No one acquainted with *The Deserted Village* could avoid recalling
it as he reads *Connecticut River,*[192] which won the *Token*
prize.

Fair River! not unknown to classic song;—

it begins; and, following Goldsmith in thought as well as
rhythm,

> See, toward yon dome where village science dwells
> When the church-clock its warning summons swells,
> What tiny feet the well-known path explore,
> And gaily gather from each rustic door. . . .
> Scorn not this lowly race, ye sons of pride,
> Their joys disparage, nor their hopes deride.

In the concluding stanza the emigrants have come, not
from fair Auburn, but from their Connecticut village to
the

> western wilds, which thronging hordes explore,
> Or ruder Erie's serpent-haunted shore,

though the same mother is soothing the same babes with
the same tales of home. *The Ancient Mariner* reappears
as *The Disobedient Son*,[193] who went to sea without his
parents' permission. This "truant sailor-boy," as he
calls himself, suffers more lurid tortures than Coleridge's
Mariner, being singed with molten lava and licked by the
red tongue of a slimy, green sea monster; but the under-
lying feeling is the same:

> Up came the dawn. With pain I raved,
>   Then like a child would weep.
> Methought it walked like Christ, who saved
>   The faithless on the deep.
>
> Up rose the clear and glorious sun,
>   Dark sea-birds clapped their wing,
> And hovered o'er me one by one,
>   As o'er a perished thing.
> A ship! A ship!—her gallant crew
>   With pride the waves did stem,
> My shrieks of anguish wilder grew,
>   What were those shrieks to them? . . .

> But lo! there came a spectre-boat,
> I hailed not—made no sign,
> Yet o'er the wave I ceased to float
> Nor felt the whelming brine.

Were it worth the pains, a similar use of "models" could be demonstrated for most of Mrs. Sigourney's productions. The poem she wrote after visiting Wordsworth is reminiscent of *The Excursion;* her verses on the sewing machine,

> Click!—Click!—Click!—
> There in a pile they lie,
> Shirts and bosoms and collars . . .[194]

could be set to the tune of Hood's *Song of the Shirt.* Occasional lines from the Spenserian stanzas of *Pocahontas,*

> Roll on, majestic flood, in power and pride![195]

or

> Out on the waters! On the deep, deep sea!
> Out, out upon the waters . . .[196]

remind one of *Childe Harold.* She was not ashamed of using well-known models. A poetical greeting sent to Longfellow on his birthday trips merrily along to the strains of *Hiawatha* while Mrs. Sigourney tells with what ardor the mountains of Maine will oppose the attempts of any other range to claim him as a native:

> We will fight, if it be needful,
> Fight with every crested hill top. . . .
> With Vermont's green knights in armor, . . .

And the rocky chiefs of Mexic,
Cordilleras, Cotapaxi,
Popocatapetl also,
Should they bar our just pretensions. . . .[197]

While it is not impossible to choose from Mrs. Hemans'
poems a stanza here and there that can be matched foot
by foot with one by Mrs. Sigourney, let us say as in these
other instances, that "the American Hemans" *drew her
inspiration* from her English prototype. The similarities
Poe criticized are found throughout the "gemmiferous"
school of poetry; and as Mrs. Sigourney is acknowledged
the "gemmiest" of them all, the characteristics deserve
to be considered at some length.

The "gemmy" poet lives in a world no ordinary mortal has ever seen, where the commonest objects bear the
most elaborate names. Buildings, for example, if very
small, are "mansions"; larger ones are "piles" or
"domes" of various styles. "Dark domes" are prisons;
"bright domes" are universities; and "holy domes" are
churches. All about these buildings beneath "umbra-
geous" trees, grow hundreds of varieties of rather metal-
lic flowers, gathered from the Alps and the Andes, the
graves of poets and of missionaries—each with a botanical name and an adjective rarely separable from it. There
one finds the "happy harebell," the "cheerful mari-
gold," the "protean sweet-william," and the "aspiring
larkspur." Many of these jewels, like the "oary-footed
duck" that pursues "the people of the pool" (strange
creatures resembling our bull frogs) and "the armèd
heel" of the small boys who "dare the frozen pool" are
drawn from well-known eighteenth-century caskets.
There is a "gemmy" ocean, too, called the "storm-

toss'd deep'' or the ''treacherous main.'' Here upon
''sapphire waves'' with ''crests of snow'' float two sizes
of ships—the smaller ones ''fragile arks,'' the larger,
''sturdy barks.'' There are just three nautical parts to a
bark: ''bowed masts,'' ''swelling sails,'' and ''slippery
shrouds,'' though a somewhat more complicated anatomy
is indicated when she holds her breath in deep astonish-
ment, or finds

> her furrowing feet
> Sealed to the curdling brine.[198]

Both types of boat are navigated by a curious race of
''seamen,'' who much prefer Bibles to rum (''Mess-
mates! Let us do without it!'')[199] whene'er they go

> To dare the whelming wave.[200]

All day long they sit in the forecastle, telling gloomy
tales of physical and moral shipwreck, and wondering
how they will ever find the graves of their little children,
usually girls between five and six, who are slowly dying
ashore.

It is perhaps this sedentary life that makes ''gemmy''
sailors such a sickly lot; at least once a day the ship's bell
tolls, and they file out to witness a burial at sea. The victim is, strangely enough, always one of the youngest of
them, who

> oft had boldly dared the slippery shrouds
> At midnight watch.[201]

No one knows what killed him; no one asks. While they
stand gazing at the pale, hollow cheek, one remembers the
blessing of his ''hoary sire'' and how the tears ''coursed

o'er his mother's cheek" when he went to sea; another seems to see the fair-haired girl who "through the woodbine of her lattice" watched "his last, far step." Still another hides in his "faithful breast"

> a bright chestnut lock, which the dead youth
> Had severed with a cold and trembling hand
> In life's extremity, and bade him bear . . .
> To his blest Mary.[202]

At this point the seamen "bow low their sunburnt faces" and sob aloud. Then the chaplain, with whom all of Mrs. Sigourney's "barks" are supplied, reads the burial service, some of which invariably creeps into the poem; there is a plunge, and the youth goes

> Down to the floor of ocean, 'mid the beds
> Of brave and beautiful ones.[203]

There, "'neath the billows" is a region as populous as the earth, strewn with young corpses and "pale pearls" the size of crab apples. In a "dome of coral," "laved by the fathomless fountains of the deep,"

> The mermaid hath twisted her fingers cold
> With the mesh of the sea-boy's curls of gold.[204]

The most remarkable thing about this "gemmy" world, however, is the way in which inanimate objects busy themselves with every sort of domestic activity. The "emerald isles" that "sleep" on the "breast" of the ocean are "cradled" in "robes of light."[205] The clouds sweep round the dying sun

> With crimson banner, and golden pall
> Like a host to their chieftain's funeral.[206]

One even reads how "winter set his frosty foot upon Spring's skirts and troubled her";[207] how the willow wands "hung out their curtains";[208] how the "rocks robed themselves in laurel, and the wild strawberry blushed as it ran to hide among the matted grass."[209] Rivers, "dressed" in "robes of silver," roam through the "breasts" of valleys, washing the "rich velvet of the curtaining banks."[210] This was the style Oliver Wendell Holmes was parodying in *Evening, by a Tailor:*

Ah me! how lovely is the golden braid
That binds the skirts of Night's descending robe! . . .
Kind Nature, shuffling in her loose undress,
Lays bare her shady bosom. . . .[211]

Mrs. Sigourney's "gemminess" was not confined to her poetry. Her prose acquired the taint during the thirties, and toward the end of her life private letters and even her diary are permeated with it. To an intimate friend she writes in all seriousness that she is at the shore for her "necessary annual inhalation of saline air," apologizing for her impeccable penmanship by saying that at the hotel "the instruments of chirography are not prone to be of the best quality, or fully available to any legible purpose."[212] Her birthday "added itself like a pearl to the necklace of life";[213] while such humble materials as sugar and butter become "saccarine and oleaginous matter."[214] The perfect euphemism, however, occurs in her autobiography, where she refers to

a quadruped member of our establishment which has not been mentioned, and is, I suppose, scarcely mentionable to ears polite. Yet I could never understand why it should be an offence to delicacy to utter the name of an animal which the Evangelists have recorded on their pages as plunging, in a dense herd, "down a steep place into the sea, and perishing in the waters."[215]

But one looks in vain through all her fifty volumes for the three-letter word ''pig.'' With such examples in mind, one reads with amazement contemporary reviews that commend Mrs. Sigourney's works for their ''entire freedom from artificiality.''

Of the many qualities for which her poems were praised the modern reader will be most likely to admit sweetness of versification. After dwelling at such length on the absurdities of her style, it is only fair to give some examples of her poetry at its best. The first is from *Pocahontas:*

> Like fallen leaves those forest-tribes have fled:
>   Deep 'neath the turf their rusted weapon lies;
> No more their harvest lifts its golden head,
>   Nor from their shaft the stricken red-deer flies:
> But from the far, far west, where holds, so hoarse,
> The lonely Oregon, its rock-strewn course,
>   While old Pacific's sullen surge replies,
> Are heard their exiled murmurings deep and low,
> Like one whose smitten soul departeth full of wo.
>
> .   .   .   .
>
> Forgotten race, farewell! Your haunts we tread,
>   Our mighty rivers speak your words of yore,
> Our mountains wear them on their misty head,
>   Our sounding cataracts hurl them to the shore;
> But on the lake your flashing oar is still,
> Hush'd is your hunter's cry on dale and hill,
>   Your arrow stays the eagle's flight no more;
> And ye, like troubled shadows, sink to rest
> In unremember'd tombs, unpitied and unbless'd.[216]

Through shabby images and threadbare phrases there
flows a smooth and sometimes melodious verse. Mrs. Sigourney's greatest facility, however, lay in blank verse;
the very ease with which it came from her pen is responsible for much of the diffuseness that mars all her
writing. The *Death of an Infant* quoted above, perhaps
because of its brevity, has often been considered her *chef
d'œuvre;* "it is enough to convert an Infidel, and to bring
tears into the eyes of the veriest misanthrope that ever
lived," said an Irish writer,[217] reviewing Mrs. Sigourney
in the respectable company of Holmes, Longfellow, and
Bryant. Of the longer poems in blank verse *To-morrow*[218]
has been often commended. This piece was written in
England, a day or two after the visit to Rydal Mount;
and both the subject and its treatment are redolent of
Wordsworth.

> . . . as the swift coach
> Stopped at its destined goal, an ancient dame
> Came from a neighboring cottage, with such speed
> As hoary years could make, and earnestly
> Scanning each passenger, with hurried tone
> Demanded, *"Is he come?"*
>   "No; not today;
> *To-morrow,"* was the answer.
>   So, back she turned,
> Lifting her shrivelled finger, with a look
> Half credulous, half-sorrowing, and still
> Repeating *"aye, to-morrow,"* homeward went. . . .

Years before her son had quarreled with his father and
joined the army; but one day the mother heard that he
was invalided home; she made his bed ready, hung a cur-
tain of flowered muslin "o'er the little casement," and
got out his late father's favorite chair.

The morning came.
Slow sped the hours; she heaped the cheerful fire
In the small grate, and ere the coach arrived
Stood, with a throbbing heart, expectant there.
"Is Willy come?" Each traveller intent
On his own business made her no reply:—
"Coachman! is Willy here?"
                    "No! No! he's dead!
Good woman! dead, and buried near the coast
Three days ago."
                    But when a stranger marked
How the strong hues of speechless misery
Changed every feature, he in pity said,
"Perhaps he'll come tomorrow."
                    Home she turned,
Struck to the heart, and wept the livelong night,
Insensible to comfort; and to those,
Who came in kind compassion to her side,
Answering nothing.
                    But when day restored
The hour of expectation, with strange zeal
She rose, and dressed, and cast her mantle on,
And as the coachman checked his foaming steeds
Stood closely by his side. "Is Willy here?
Has Willy come?" while he, by pity schooled,
Answered "to-morrow!"
                    And thus years have fled. . . .

The death of Mrs. Sigourney's first three babies at
birth undoubtedly accounts for much of the interest she
displayed in dying infants. But she soon evolved a formula for this type of poem, using it over and over again
with a monotonous similarity of metaphor. The following example is chosen quite at random:

TO A DYING INFANT

Go to thy rest, my child!
    Go to thy dreamless bed,
Gentle and undefiled,
    With blessings on thy head;
Fresh roses in thy hand,
    Buds on thy pillow laid,
Haste from this fearful land,
    Where flowers so quickly fade.

Before thy heart might learn
    In waywardness to stray,
Before thy feet could turn
    The dark and downward way;
Ere sin might wound the breast,
    Or sorrow wake the tear,
Rise to thy home of rest,
    In yon celestial sphere.

Because thy smile was fair,
    Thy lip and eye so bright,
Because thy cradle-care
    Was such a fond delight,
Shall Love with weak embrace
    Thy heavenward flight detain?
No! Angel, seek thy place
    Amid yon cherub-train.[219]

The spirit floating skyward became the favorite ending
for all her poems; one tries as in a sort of game to foresee
how poems called *The Gift of a Bible, The Conflagration
at New York, The Ancient Family Clock,* and *To the
Cactus Speciosissimus* can possibly be brought around to
the same conclusion. They all are. Thackeray, with his

keen sense of the ridiculous, caught the formula and parodied it:

> As Mrs. Sigourney sweetly sings:—
>   'Oh the soul is a soft and a delicate thing:
>   The soul is a lute with a thrilling string,
>   A spirit that floats on a gossamer's wing.'[220]

To be called "the American Hemans" was not the highest praise Mrs. Sigourney received. In 1842 a friend[221] reviewing *Pocahontas* declared that "if her powers of expression were equal to the purity and elevation of her habits of thought and feeling, she would be a female Milton, or a Christian Pindar!" This equivocal compliment, though it meant little to Mrs. Sigourney's readers, many of whom had never heard of the heathen Pindar, increased her fame among the uncritical book buyers whose favor provided her income. Before one can understand how her extraordinary reputation was achieved, he must know something of the character of the people for whom she wrote.

They were first of all ardent patriots, still conscious of the Revolution and anxious to have their literature as independent as their government from that of England. In the early years of the nation, one fiery person, according to Lowell, even advocated the adoption of a "lingo of our own, to be called the Columbian or Hesperian."[222] Most people, however, were content to read the English language so long as American subjects were chosen. But it was generally felt that no nation could be really respectable without a distinctly national literature. After viewing the scenes of the *Æneid*, an American friend wrote Mrs. Sigourney in 1832:

Shall my own native land with all her treasures be left unsung because no bard can be found with his magic touch to immortalize her story? . . . Think of this dear Mrs Sigourney, and when you next write me, tell me that you have selected for the subject of your song some event connected with American Story. Our authors should rise above the mean imitation of taking their subjects from a foreign country. They will never be respected or read in Europe unless they make a literature of their own.[223]

This feeling was shared by the smallest countries. A missionary to Africa wrote in 1836:

Liberia's Muse has not yet awaked from her torpor, . . . but we look forward to the day . . . when she shall tune her lyre to notes, that shall not be heard with contempt, even by the Bards of other climes.[224]

Independence alone would not satisfy these lofty souls. The size and resources of the new continent seemed to demand a literature commensurate with them in grandeur; if that little dribble of an Avon produced a Shakespeare, they argued, what a giant might we not expect from along the Mississippi![225] Poets, who, of course, had never seen it, wrote thundering apostrophes to the Father of Waters. Mrs. Hale's lines[226] express the general sentiment enthusiastically:

> Monarch of Rivers in the wide domain
> Where Freedom writes her signature in stars,
> And bids her Eagle bear the blazing scroll
> To usher in the reign of peace and love,
> Thou mighty Mississippi!—may my song
> Swell with thy power . . .

The following pages trace the stream through a romantic course of rocky cañons and snow-capped peaks

> Where Liberty has found a Pisgah height.

Then in a burst of patriotism, the author exclaims:

Ay, gather Europe's royal Rivers all—

the "snow-swelled Neva," the "dark Danube," the "castled Rhine," the "rushing Rhone," the "yellow Tiber,"

> And Seine, where Fashion glasses fairest forms,
> And Thames that bears the riches of the world:—
> Gather their waters in one ocean mass,
> —Our Mississippi, rolling proudly on
> Would sweep them from its path, or swallow up
> Like Aaron's rod, these streams of fame and song.

In much the same way, it was felt, our literature would swallow up all others if only it could be produced in sufficient quantity.

This confusion of patriotism with literature was one of the forces that prevented criticism. Another was acceptance of the principle that the religious or moral note automatically placed a poem above criticism. Thus: Mrs. Sigourney's *Niagara* "is sufficient to establish her fame as a poetess of the first rank. It does more and better than this; it stamps her as the devoted Christian."[227] The "critics" themselves were whole-hearted believers in the ethical purpose of literature. The *North American Review*, the ruling power in 1835, declared:

> The true and only worthy object of literary effort, and all scientific research is, to purify the heart while they enlarge the mind, and thus render both . . . worthy of the Source to which they owe their powers. . . .[228]

Poetry's "worthy office" in this scheme is that of

withdrawing the mind from the earthly and material to fix it on that which is spiritual and undying.[229] . . . The writer, who expects the future generations to rise up and call him blessed, who would add his name to those of the great benefactors of mankind, whose memory shall not fail, must inscribe it on the rock of ages.[230]

Mrs. Sigourney's work was all of this lithographic nature; and while she has not enjoyed the perpetuity predicted, she did succeed better than any of her predecessors in pleasing the reading public of her time.

Brought up on *Poor Richard,* Americans worshiped respectability and material success. To them Mrs. Sigourney appealed strongly as the poor girl who had grown famous. Everyone knew of "her romantic marriage with the wealthy and scholarly merchant, Mr. Sigourney"; pictures of their "magnificent" house were often published with accounts of her career; her reception by "the crowned heads of Europe" was evolved by a popular imagination, which delighted to represent Monarchy prostrate at the feet of Republican Genius. And whatever one may think of her poetry, he cannot deny that with very limited ability she made herself one of the most famous persons of her day. Few critics, indeed, dared judge her work apart from her person. "A woman," Poe remarked, "will never be brought to admit a non-identity between herself and her book";[231] and no well-bred man would give himself the liberty to speak ill of women. Mrs. Stephens, staunchest of puffers, expresses the feeling of Mrs. Sigourney's admirers:

I write more of the woman than the authoress, because had the woman been less perfect, the author had never been reverenced as she is reverenced. She still lives the first pure impersonation of an American literary lady. In her life you find no distorted acts, no wild search after unattainable sympathies and transcendental delusions. She never degrades her genius with sophistry, or sullies the ermine that nature has cast about her, by allowing one sentiment which angels might not acknowledge, to find meritorious beauty in her genius. She is emphatically a great, good woman.[232]

More often than not it was the *woman* rather than the *authoress* that wrote her poems. The domestic note is heard again and again. She took the public into her confidence on her children's birthdays or when she had to move from the great "mansion."

Her illnesses were chronicled by brother and sister poets in the press. Hearing that she was "languishing under the affliction of a very threatening disease," one gentleman wrote an obituary poem, which, with cheerful reference to her book, he named "*Pleasant Memories of a Sweet Poetess* (Mrs. L. H. Sigourney)."

> The harp of the minstrel is mute,
>   The spirit has gone to its rest:
> There is sorrow and sighing on earth
>   And joy in the land of the blest.
>
> .   .   .   .   .   .
>
> Adieu! sweetest minstrel adieu!
>   Oh! when shall such other arise?
> What seraph shall take up her song
>   As she wings her bright way to the skies?[233]

He added a note to the effect that, if she should recover, her friends "may still receive it as what might, in a more adverse event, have constituted a posthumous, though very inadequate, tribute to her estimable and cherished memory." Then, learning of her recovery, he was kind enough to send her the verses, and was rewarded with a letter from the sweet minstrel, who hoped she was "not wholly ungrateful for being spared to read what was essentially elegiac.''[234] Such personal bits as these kept Mrs. Sigourney before her public—a public composed largely of ladies as patriotic, romantic, and pious as herself.

All during the forties and fifties famous visitors to America stopped in Hartford to pay their respects to the American Hemans. George Combe, the phrenologist, brought his wife, a niece of Mrs. Siddons; Ole Bull, the Norwegian violinist came; even the great Dickens called to express his appreciation of the charming lines Mrs. Sigourney had written for the banquet the night before, and did her, perhaps, a kindness by failing to record his impression in *American Notes*. Fredrika Bremer, the Swedish authoress, has left an account of her visit in December, 1849.

We were invited for the evening to Mrs. Sigourney, the author of *Pleasant Memories from Pleasant Lands,* and here I shook hands with the whole town, I believe, from the bishop, a handsome prelate, to the school-girl, and played my usual part in society. Mrs. Sigourney, a very kind little sentimentalist, but a very agreeable lady, dressed in green, about fifty years old, with a good motherly demeanor, would perforce keep me all night, and I could not return to my excellent chamber at the hotel, which I would so gladly have done, where I might have rested and been silent. In the morning, however, I forgot the little annoyance in breakfast and conversation with my kind hostess and her pleasant only daughter. The sun shone into the room, and the whole had the character of a good home made warm with love. . . . At parting she presented me with a handsome volume of her collected poetical works, and therein I read a poem called *Our Country,* for which I had to kiss her hand, so beautiful, so noble, and so truly feminine was the spirit it breathed.[235]

The good people of Hartford were proud of their own poetess, whom these illustrious personages found worthy of honor. They liked to think that this modest little lady, who attended so regularly the meetings of the Charitable Society and sewed and knit and chatted like one of themselves, was at the same time ''the confidential correspondent of Hannah More—a friend of Joanna Baillie and the Countess of Blessington—the recipient of costly gifts from Royalty in honor of her Muse—the most famous of the female bards of her country.''

With the American nobility Mrs. Sigourney maintained closer relations. She kept a large calendar book in which were listed the anniversaries of their births and marriages, and other events worthy of record. It is faintly amusing to find, in turning over the dozens of faded, carefully saved letters from Presidents, Governors, Generals, and other public figures, how many of them express naïve surprise that the inevitable ''volume'' has ''happened to arrive'' on his birthday. Still, her sympathies were broad: the book held many humbler names.

Is my recollection correct [she wrote an acquaintance], . . . that your little Robert's birth-day was May 6th If so, my letter is dated on the second anniversary of his entrance, upon this beautiful & changeful state of existence. Please make agreeable to him, my good wishes, and congratulations on this domestic epoch.[236]

Just how to convey to two-year-old Robert the good wishes of a person he had never seen must have puzzled the parent.

Some of Mrs. Sigourney's presentations were made with deliberate intention of securing autographs. Her friends, knowing her reputation as ''confidential corre-

spondent'' of the great, often appealed to her for letters.
There were occasional disappointments. A gentleman
begged her to get him an autograph of Fitz-Greene Hal-
leck.

I immediately wrote him [she said], and to make more sure
of a reply, sent him one of the very best of my poor volumes.
But I over-rated the chivalry of the gifted poet, and after
looking many months for a snip of his chirography, which I
should at once have transmitted to your collection of autographs, am compelled to confess that I have failed to procure
it.[237]

The flowery letters that accompanied these presentations
did not always have just exactly the effect she intended:
Mrs. Browning quotes with some amusement Mrs. Sigourney's remark that ''the sound of my poetry is stirring
the 'deep green forests of the New World.' ''[238] But the
fact that she was quite unknown never deterred her from
writing. Even while she was conducting the school during her first years in Hartford she began sending utter
strangers ''a few verses called forth'' by a death in the
family,[239] or some other melancholy incident. As her
reputation grew, she was besieged with requests for
poems for every conceivable occasion—consecrations, or-
dinations, installations, holiday services, wedding anniversaries, wooings. But the most frequent appeals—appeals both pathetic and ludicrous—were for elegies and
epitaphs. A stranger writes saying that his wife was
likely to die, and had a young babe; he would like ''some
poetry to be written in such a way that it would answer
for mother and child, should both be taken by death.''[240]
Another, also unknown, whose son had died at the age of
nine months, weighing just thirteen pounds, requested

"some poetry to be framed, glazed, and hung over the chimney-piece, to keep the other children from forgetting him.'"²⁴¹ With many of these requests she complied; and being so continually approached by those unknown to her, it may have seemed natural in turn to bestow her works upon strangers. The profits from some of her books were completely absorbed by the copies she bought for presentation; and in one case she printed the whole first edition at her own cost to give away. But the practice arose from generous motives, surely, and it should be considered as a gratification of personal vanity rather than a form of advertising.

Yet she certainly did not neglect her reputation. The magazines to which she contributed always noticed her books with kindly, or even extravagant approval, simply as an act of friendly interest. But if they neglected it, Mrs. Sigourney was not above inquiring into the reason. The *North American Review,* which corresponded in a way to the Edinburgh reviews, had for some years persistently ignored her works; and finally, in 1845, just after the publication of *Scenes in My Native Land,* she wrote William H. Prescott, the historian, to solicit his help.

I have but a slight acquaintance with Mr. Bowes [he replied], who is both editor & proprietor of the N A Review; and, indeed as he lives at Cambridge, have not set eyes on him these two years or more. But my relations with him are very friendly & I shall be most happy if I can be useful to you in this matter. It certainly was a great oversight in him not to have made your popular works the subject of an express article; but his attention, I suppose, is more immediately called to the votaries of Apollo in his own neighborhood—a lame reason.

I think the best way will be for me to present him a copy (if you will authorize me) in your name, & I will write to him to draw his attention to this publication, urging your undoubted claims, & requesting him to have them fairly canvassed in his journal. It will give me great pleasure to do this; & if his silence has proceeded from accident, as probable, my application may have some effect.

But whether it has or has not, is, after all, of but little moment to one in your position. Your country has long since passed upon your literary claims, & has given you a name among her children—as you must be well aware—that is to form part of the National inheritance to all future times.[242]

The volume was received and listed; but no comment was made on it.

American reviews of the time affected a classical, scholarly air. They were at their best discussing Milman's *History of Christianity,* or such works as *The Manners and Customs of the Japanese in the Nineteenth Century,* or Hallam's *Introduction to the Literary History of Europe.* Mrs. Sigourney's best poems, written for the heart rather than the intellect, made little impression on their pages. It was perhaps vanity that tempted her occasionally to an ostentatious parade of French or Latin that often betrayed her. *Delendo est Carthago* may have been a typographical error; false accents in botanical names could be forgiven; but *Diem Perdida*—"I have lost a day"[243]—recurring in each stanza of a poem of the same title aroused the critics' wrath. Pointing out that the word should be *Perdidi* and the accent on the first syllable, one of them remarked that a lady was not expected to be acquainted with Latin. "If, however, she choose to introduce words of a language she does not understand, she is not entirely free from blame, if she neglect to procure the advice of persons better qualified than herself.''[244] Why had she not procured the advice of Mr. Sigourney, whose rare classical attainments were so well known?

But rebukes from learned quarterlies had little effect on the sales of her books. Her readers, neither scholarly nor critical, were more concerned with sentiment than with Latin quantities. Pious reviews like the one that declared her *Letters to Young Ladies* would ''prove a solace in the cottage of poverty, and form a gem in the libraries of wealth'' did most to spread her reputation far and wide at home and abroad.

The young, green West [Mrs. Sigourney wrote to Lady Blessington] is inclined to appreciate genius and taste. . . .[245] We are, as you doubtless know, emphatically a *reading people*. Our magazines, and many of the works that they announce, go into the humble dwelling of the manufacturer, into the brown hand of the farmer, into the log-hut of the emigrant who sees around him the dark forms of the remnant of our aboriginal tribes, . . . hears the murmurs of the turbid Missouri, perhaps the breaking billows of the Pacific.[246]

These people formed Mrs. Sigourney's most enthusiastic audience. Many a letter reached her from settlers in the wilds of Ohio or Michigan, expressing with clumsy sincerity the comfort her verses had given in the tragic hour when death entered the log hut of the emigrant. In the grim struggle against the wilderness, poetry offered an escape from reality. Here, if anywhere, it was good to be reminded that death was a blessing in disguise. Here the pious infant, precociously moral, the pale heroine with her spotless soul, the honest toiler, brushing a tear from his bronzed cheek, the venerable, white-haired parent— were preparing the generation that was to welcome *A*

Psalm of Life and *The Village Blacksmith* in the next decade.

Mrs. Sigourney practiced constantly in her own life the lessons of sobriety, thrift, patience, and virtue that her poems taught. She won fame by putting into words the thoughts of mute millions, too busy with their household tasks to have much time for thought. Unlike the "grand old masters," her works were "comprehensible to all," "no thought was required to read them." This is still the qualification for a popular poet: to echo conventional truisms in simple and tuneful words. The trade the newspaper poets are carrying on so prosperously today, Mrs. Sigourney began a century ago. And when the inevitable decline of her reputation set in, it came, not from any deterioration in the quality of her verse, but from the changing taste of the public.

CHAPTER FIVE

THE *LITERATI*

THE leading American magazines of the forties—
Godey's *Lady's Book,* the *Ladies' Companion,* and
Graham's—competed for the exclusive use of Mrs.
Sigourney's name; but none of them quite succeeded in
obtaining it. Godey, with whom in 1839 she had made a
contract to that end, found great difficulty in persuading
her that it was wrong to allow the *Companion* the privilege at the same time.[247] Mrs. Sigourney, as a matter of
fact, did no real editing for either. Although she was
listed on the title-page, the actual work of the *Lady's
Book* was performed by her friend Mrs. Sarah J. Hale.
Pioneers in the trade of literature, the two women had
been drawn together by mutual interests ever since 1828,
when Mrs. Hale printed articles on the Greek relief
movement in her *American Ladies' Magazine;* and they
became such fast friends that when she published *Traits
of American Life,* in 1835, she dedicated it to Mrs. Sigourney, as a token of the ''esteem and affection cherished
for her by the author.'' Together they had served as hon-
orary members of The Association for the Mutual Improvement of Female Teachers, organized by Mrs. Willard in 1837.[248] On her trips between Boston and New
York, Mrs. Hale, who was intimate with the family, often
stopped in Hartford.

While Mrs. Sigourney was abroad, Mrs. Hale, in her gossipy way, kept the readers of the *Lady's Book* informed of her triumphs:

We perceive it stated in several of our papers that one of our editors, Mrs. Lydia H. Sigourney, is attracting much attention in Paris, and is deservedly very popular. In a letter to ourselves, dated at Paris, she mentions her intention of publishing Pocahontas and other poems in London.[249]

The next issue, soon after Mrs. Sigourney's return, recounted the results of her travels:

Mrs. Sigourney. Our readers will, we are sure, be happy to learn that this lady has lately returned from her visit to Europe, and with her widely extended circle of correspondence and other facilities will be able to promote greatly, what she has much at heart, the continued interest and improvement of the Lady's Book. She has brought with her an admirable story by Mrs. S. C. Hall—the celebrated illustrator of Ireland—which Mr. Hall, her husband, pronounces the most spirited thing she has written in some time. Mary Russell Mitford, author of "Our Village," has also promised a sketch, which we presume will be in time for the July number. Other transatlantic arrangements have been made which will be duly announced.[250]

It is to be feared that the mysterious "other transatlantic arrangements" proved something of a disappointment to the staff of the *Lady's Book*. Mrs. Hall's admirable story turned out to be a commonplace little sketch of two scant pages; and they had advertised it as the first work of this talented lady to appear in an American periodical, only to be informed, "though not in the most courteous manner" that she had contributed previously to a rival. A poem by Maria Edgeworth was then announced.

She informed Mrs. Sigourney when giving it to her, that it was almost the only poetry she ever wrote in her life. Mrs. S. in a letter to us says—"She gave it to me in her own hand writing as a keepsake. She is one of the most delightful women in conversation I have ever met, and as a friend is invaluable."[251]

The twelve prosaic lines, when they appeared,[252] explained clearly why Miss Edgeworth rarely wrote poetry. Another poem telling the regret of a certain *Amelia* at Mrs. Sigourney's departure from London, though excellent advertising for the talented editor, was rather dull reading for subscribers. But the greatest cause for dissatisfaction the *Lady's Book* found was that Mrs. Sigourney, in spite of contract and liberal remuneration, insisted on giving the *Companion* nearly as many poems as she gave her own magazine.

This unfriendly procedure may be explained in part by the relations between the two lady editors. Mrs. Sigourney deeply distrusted Mrs. Hale. Just why, one cannot say. Perhaps the feeling began in 1839 when Mrs. Hale had rather openly sided against Mrs. Willard in her marital difficulties. She forms a frequent subject in Mrs. Willard's letters to Mrs. Sigourney;[253] but the cause of the dislike is nowhere clearly defined. Mrs. Sigourney herself kept up a cordial correspondence with her dear "co-labourer" in the *Lady's Book;* yet behind every derogatory notice of her works, she instantly suspected the malign influence of Mrs. Hale. Her suspicion reached a climax in 1841 when Rufus Griswold was preparing his *Poets and Poetry of America.* Griswold sought help from many sources; and Horace Greeley, who had occasionally published Mrs. Sigourney's verses in the *New Yorker,* promised an account of her life. Just where he secured his information is not clear; but in a letter to Griswold dated November 13, 1841,[254] he says: "I shall try to plaster over Mrs. Sigourney tomorrow; but you know how bad a job it is. As it won't do to say a word of her *real* history, how will it be possible to say *any* think? . . ." Four days later he writes: "I have just done up Mrs. Sigourney by neglecting my own business entirely. . . . This isn't good biography; I've lost the list of her works, but that is no loss at all. The biography is less humdrum without it. You can carve and plaster to suit your taste. . . ."[255] Then, with shameless duplicity, Greeley wrote Mrs. Sigourney, on March 7, 1842, just before the book was published, pretending to be displeased at the way Griswold had treated her.

I have today seen Griswold, and some sheets of his book. It is to be published on or before the 1st of April. It will be an excellent collection of American Poetry, though not quite so full as was at first intended—perhaps 550 pages. I think its value is marred, however, by a series of brief criticisms on the several authors, which are generally harsh or grudging, especially towards the Female Poets. I remarked that yourself and Miss H. F. Gould are especially touched unkindly; a brief sketch of your life and writings which I had been *requested* to furnish being thrown out, and a briefer of different tenor substituted. I doubt not but this criticism is honest, yet it has caused me some pain in view of the anxiety I felt that the notice of your writings should have been different. Griswold is so determined a contemner of the intellectual equality of Men and Women that I think he has hardly commended any Female Poet save Maria E. Brooks. I do not so much regret this in your case, since the Selections from your writings are essentially those I had indicated, and are a sufficient refutation of any disparaging prologue. The great fault of Mr. Griswold consists in attempting criticism at all when his readers had the means of judging before them. Something too much of this!

Yours,

HORACE GREELEY.

Mrs. Greeley, in poor health, would gladly be remembered.[256]

Never suspecting Greeley's treachery, Mrs. Sigourney's first thought on reading this letter was that Mrs. Hale had been pouring poison into Griswold's ear; and she wrote at once to inquire about the matter.

I received yours several days since [Greeley replied on March 16], and have seen Griswold meantime, though that was needless. I was morally certain, from circumstances well known to me, that his adverse leaning was in no wise attributable to any extraneous influence whatever; and I easily learned, by casual inquiry on meeting him, that *he has not seen or heard from Mrs. H. within a year,* if ever. You will be sure I am right as to the main fact, when I assure you that *Mrs. H. is not placed in the list of American Poets at all,* and only one of her pieces ('The Light of Home,') inserted in the appendix,[257] which is made up of occasional good effusions from Americans *not* Poets. Of course no more need be said on that head. . . .

He then explains Griswold's criticism of the female poets on the ground of "constitutional severity"; for, all of them,

saving one or two Brookses and perhaps Miss Gould are treated coldly in his volume—you perhaps as well as any and better than almost any. He excused himself to me for not inserting my notice of your life and writings by saying he had *lost* or mislaid it—which I inferred he had done purposely, and which I preferred to have done rather than have it altered. As it is, I think the extracts embodied in his work will overbear the critique. Believe me, I have done what I could to have it otherwise; and perhaps I should feel satisfied that it is no worse though I am not. The Miss Davidsons are very calmly tomohawked, and so of others.

Yours truly,

HORACE GREELEY.

This book will be really *the* American Poets—nothing before equal to it. This makes me more regret that the criticism appears harsher than justice requires.[258]

Perhaps she was wrong in suspecting Mrs. Hale, Mrs. Sigourney thought. And to soothe her conscience she sat down and wrote her a long letter telling about the throat trouble that had bothered so, and sent an intimate little message from Mary to her daughter.[259] But the dark suspicion lingered on; and before the end of the year, as a result of some unfriendly action on the part of Mrs. Hale, which is now happily forgotten (though Mrs. Willard referred to it indignantly four years later),[260] Mrs. Sigourney severed her connection with the *Lady's Book*.

The *Ladies' Companion* had the reputation of giving authors the highest prices and paying most promptly. Mrs. Sigourney's willingness to supply it with occasional articles had aroused Mr. Godey's wrath; now within a few months of their parting he saw her name placed on the title-page of the *Companion* as editor.[261] In this new position Mrs. Sigourney found two serious disadvantages: Mr. Snowden, the owner and real editor, had also a half interest in the Bowery Theater, whose performances were puffed in each issue, and the general tone of the *Companion* tended to be sensational rather than moral. Mrs. Embury, the other lady of known piety whose name guaranteed the respectability of the magazine, was pessimistic when Mrs. Sigourney proposed historic tales instead of the exciting stories then running— *The Mystery of Marie Roget*, and Mrs. Embury's own

Flora Lester, or Scenes in the Life of a Belle ("for the pale governess was no other than the once idolized belle").[262] The tone of the magazine "ought to be and might be greatly elevated," Mrs. Embury admitted; but "with Mr. Snowden's views, I doubt very much whether he would be satisfied with a series of historic tales."

I am disposed to believe [she continued] that if anything could induce him to omit the theatrical reviews it would be the assurance from you that their insertion injured the circulation of the Companion in New England. I have understood that Mr. S. is or has been interested in a pecuniary point of view in such matters, and if so, it will be only by convincing him that it is for his advantage to banish them, we can hope to influence him.

In conclusion she suggests as contributors Mrs. Seba Smith, author of *The Sinless Child,* whom there is every reason for aiding in her exertions to provide for a very lovely family, and Mr. Tuckerman, "whose poetry is as pure and high-toned as his own character."[263]

At Mrs. Sigourney's behest Mrs. Embury then wrote Mr. Snowden, explaining their views with regard to the *Companion,* stating the necessity of some "female supervision" over each issue, and proffering her services. But he did not answer her letter. "Neglect augurs ill, I fear, for our plans," she told Mrs. Sigourney. "As Mr. Snowden does not seem disposed to allow any authority for which we have not stipulated, I do not see how we are to satisfy either the public or our own consciences in this matter."[264] There is no record of how Mrs. Sigourney satisfied her conscience. It may have been through the unquestionably moral articles she contributed to the *Companion* during 1843. But whatever tranquillity she enjoyed was short lived. In the January number (which came out a week before Christmas), Snowden printed an atrocious libel on Park Benjamin, editor of the rival *New World*. The details of the quarrel are of no moment now; but the vulgar and disgusting attack in a publication that bore the mild names of Mrs. Sigourney and Mrs. Embury caused a sensation at the time. More than a year before, while the affair was smoldering, Snowden had spoken of Benjamin as "a literary hedge-hog."[265] Now he elaborated the idea, adding such epithets as "reptile," "scorpion," and "literary scarabæus." With brutal reference to the peculiarities of Benjamin's physical appearance he wrote: "We have often been told by eye-witnesses that whenever the poor creature is so unfortunate as to catch a glimpse of his disgusting form reflected in a mirror, he foams horribly at the mouth and pours forth savage imprecations upon all the human race." In keeping silence before, he concluded, "we only consulted the wishes of our thousands of readers, the dignity of the press generally, and the well-being of those talented ladies who are associated with us in the Editorial management of the Magazine."[266]

Mrs. Ann Stephens, who had worked for Snowden and most of the other editors of the day, was at this time editing *Peterson's Magazine;* and the Benjamin attack suggested a means of stealing Mrs. Sigourney from the *Companion*.

There will be a trial [she wrote Mrs. Sigourney]—Mr. Benjamin will plead his own cause of this I am certain and this abuse is so ungentlemanly, so brutal that your name—so good so pure and so sacred to your friends *must not be brought in any connection with it*—Trust me my dear Madam—must I not say my friend for you have ever been a dear and good one to me—there is but one way to avoid this. Write a letter to Mr

Benjamin for publication—disclaiming all knowledge of and participation in this coarse and cruel attack—and at the time withdraw your name from a work which will be inevitably disgraced.[267]

A letter from Benjamin had reached her before Mrs. Stephens'. As she read it the horrid thought burst suddenly upon her: in lending her name as editor she was responsible for every word published in the magazine! She had never been able to prevail on Mr. Snowden to use the *Companion* to uplift the nation by combining the Good and the Beautiful. And now her reputation was most lamentably at stake. She was technically at fault. So she wrote Benjamin a very humble letter, appealing to his chivalry, but not offering to leave the *Companion;* and in the next issue of the *New World*[268] he devoted a long editorial to the affair:

. . . Having fully resolved to seek redress in the Courts of Law, we should have made no allusion to the topic whatever, were it not requisite to disabuse the public of the idea that so highly honored a lady as Mrs. Sigourney had any manner of connection with the Ladies' Companion, except as a contributor, although she strangely enough permits her name to be used as Editor, which she is not, any more than the most insignificant poetaster, who figures in the pages of that periodical. Since, however, she permits her name to be thus used, (for the purpose, as we suppose, of attracting subscribers,) she is legally responsible for any slanderous articles, which her associate, Mr. W. W. Snowden, may choose to insert.

Mrs. Sigourney has written us a letter, dated Hartford Dec. 21, 1843, in which she concludes thus:

"I think it cannot be necessary for me to add, how truly I am grieved that any work in which I have been at all interested, should cast aspersions upon one whose talents are so widely appreciated, and whose personal friendship, from his college-days, has been highly valued by yours, with respect and regard,

L. H. SIGOURNEY."

In the rather patronizing tone that his triumph perhaps warranted, Benjamin went on to express his high opinion of Mrs. Sigourney, whose literary interests he had tried to promote as best he could. She had never seen the libel until he had called it to her attention.

We therefore exonerate the lady from all blame, except that which her connection with the magazine implies—and we shall require no further explanation from her, unless this statement shall be called into question, either publicly or privately. . . . [Mrs. Sigourney writes] that her duties in this Magazine do not comprise "that of the reception or revision of articles." Therefore she is but a simple contributor, as she is to several other periodicals. She is not *morally*, though (by allowing herself to be published as Editor, when she is not such,) she is *legally* responsible for any slanderous defamation of private character which may appear in its columns. . . .

But neither Mrs. Stephens' tearful solicitation nor Park Benjamin's public rebukes won Mrs. Sigourney to their magazines; and while her name disappeared from the title-page of the *Companion,* her contributions continued as numerous as ever.

In 1841 when *Graham's Magazine* was founded by a combination of the *Casket* and the *Gentleman's Magazine,* it was placed under the editorial supervision of Poe; and in less than a year it rose, as the *Messenger* had done, to a position of leadership among American periodicals. Poe contributed many of his finest tales to *Graham's,* but the unparalleled increase from five to twenty-five thousand subscribers was due more to his indefatigable zeal in securing the most popular authors of the day as contributors and Mr. Graham's generosity in paying them. With the single exception of Irving, every prominent American writer was represented in *Graham's* during the forties. But no magazine in those years could pretend to the *best* writers without including Mrs. Sigourney; and Poe wrote to her thus:

PHILADELPHIA. Nov. 10. 1841

DEAR MADAM,

Since my connexion, as editor, with "Graham's Magazine," of this city, I have been sadly disappointed to find that you deem us unworthy your correspondence. Month after month elapses, and, although our list numbers "good names," we still miss that of Mrs Sigourney. Is there no mode of tempting you to send us an occasional contribution? Mr Graham desires me to say that he would be *very especially* obliged if you could furnish him with a poem, however brief, for the January number. His compensation—for the days of gratuitous contributions are luckily gone by—will be at least as liberal as that of any publisher in America. May I hope to hear from you in reply? Excuse, dear Madam, this villanous steel pen, and believe me with high respect

Y^r Mo ob S^t.

EDGAR A POE

Mrs L. H. Sigourney.[269]

The apology for the "villanous steel pen" was quite superfluous; for this polite note, with its graceful flattery, so different from the fulsome compliment of most editors, was written in a "chirography" that fairly shamed Mrs. Sigourney's own perfect hand. There was, however, an apology that would have pleased her more: for six years she had been inwardly rankling under Poe's charges of imitation and chicanery. So she took pains in acceding to his request to point out the curious inconsist-

Philadelphia. Nov. 10. 1841.

Dear Madam,

Since my connexion, as editor, with
Grahams Magazine, of this city, I have been sadly
disappointed to find that you deem us unworthy
your correspondence. Month after month elapses,
and, although our list numbers "good names," we
still miss that of Mrs Sigourney. Is there no mode
of tempting you to send us an occasional contribution? Mr Graham desires me to say that he
would be very especially obliged if you could furnish him with a poem, however brief, for the January number. His compensation — for the days of
gratuitous contributions are luckily gone by — will
be at least as liberal as that of any publisher in
America. May I hope to hear from you in reply?
Excuse, dear Madam, this villanous steel pen, and
believe me with high respect

Yr mo obt

Edgar A Poe

Mrs L. H. Sigourney.

Facsimile of a Letter to Mrs. Sigourney from Edgar Allan Poe
By Permission of The Connecticut Historical Society.

ency between his former strictures and his present sad
disappointment. Perhaps he would examine her new volume, *Pocahontas,* to see if she has improved. Does he
know who is now writing the reviews for the *Messenger?*

PHILADELPHIA. Nov. 16. 1842*

DEAR MADAM,

I hasten to reply to yours of the 13th, and to thank you for
your consent in the matter of contribution to our January
number. We are forced to go to press at a very early period—
for our edition is, *in reality,* twenty-five thousand—so that it
would be desirable we should have your article in hand by the
1st December. We shall look for it with much anxiety, as we are
using every exertion to prepare a number of more than ordinary attraction. So far, we have been quite successful. We
shall have papers from Longfellow, Benjamin, Willis, Fay,
Herbert, Mrs Stephens, Mrs Embury, Dr Reynell Coates, and
(what will surprise you) from Sergeant Talfourd, author of
"Ion"—besides others of nearly equal celebrity.

Is it not possible that we can make an arrangement with
yourself for an article *each* month? It would give us the greatest pleasure to do so; and the terms of Mr Graham will be at
least *as* liberal as those of any publisher. Shall we hear from
you upon this point?

I regret that I am unable to answer your query touching the
"Messenger":—nor do I believe it answerable. Since my seces-
sion, I *think* that Mr White has had no regular editor. He de-
pends pretty much upon *chance,* for assistance in the conduct
of the Magazine—sometimes procuring aid from Mr James E.
Heath, of Richmond—sometimes (but not of late days) from
Judge Beverly Tucker, author of "George Balcombe." Mr Benjamin has occasionally furnished him with editorial or rather,

---

* This is an obvious slip for 1841. The articles mentioned in the
letter appear in *Graham's* for January, 1842.

critical matters, and Mr R. W. Griswold has lately written
much for the Magazine.

> I am, Dear Madam,
>> With the highest respect,
>>> Y^r ob. S^t.
>>>> EDGAR A POE

Mrs L. H. Sigourney

Sergeant Talfourd's sonnet, expressing the pious wish
that his son may

> through the vista of long years embrace
> Without a blush his first Etonian hour,

heads the great January number. Longfellow's contribution was *The Goblet of Life;* Park Benjamin sent two
poems; and Lowell, a song beginning "Violet! sweet violet!" Mrs. Sigourney's *To a Land Bird at Sea* shares
a page with Mrs. Welby's *Lines Written on a Portrait of
William Henry Harrison.* But she found a far deeper
satisfaction in a short review of *Pocahontas* that appeared on the last page:

Some years ago we had occasion to speak of "Zinzendorf,
and Other Poems," by Mrs. Sigourney, and at that period we
found, or fancied that we found many points, in her general
manner, which called for critical animadversion. At *no* period,
however, have we been so rash as to dispute her claim to high
rank among the poets of the land. In the volume now published by the Messieurs Harper, we are proud to discover *not
one* of those more important blemishes which were a stain upon
her early style. We have accused her of imitation of Mrs.
Hemans—but this imitation is no longer apparent. . . .
"Pocahontas" is a far finer poem than a late one on the same
subject by Mrs. Seba Smith. Mrs. Sigourney, however, has the
wrong accentuation of Powhatan. In the second stanza of the

poem, too, "harassed" is in false quantity. We speak of these trifles merely *en passant*.

Hereafter we may speak in full.[270]

But the regular monthly contributions Poe proposed were never arranged. In April, 1842, for reasons that have never been satisfactorily explained, Poe resigned, and was succeeded by Rufus Griswold.

Griswold's *Poets and Poetry of America* had just appeared. Mrs. Sigourney's hand trembled as she scanned the table of contents for the notice Greeley had so thoughtfully warned her of. Following a brief and inaccurate account of her life, she found the bitter words.

MRS. SIGOURNEY has surpassed any of the poets of her sex in this country in the extent of her productions; and their religious and domestic character has made them popular with the large classes who regard more than artistic merit the spirit and tendency of what they read. Her subjects are varied, and her diction generally melodious and free; but her works are written too carelessly; they lack vigour and condensation; and possess but few of the elements of enduring verse. . . .[271]

As in the case of so many other dead ladies embalmed in "Griswold's Graveyard," the modern critic finds this epitaph a just one. It was not the charge of carelessness that hurt Mrs. Sigourney most; she knew that many of her poems could be improved if she had time to work over them. The hardest blow was that the Rev. Rufus Griswold, the Baptist clergyman, whose own life was divided between literature and religion, should so scornfully separate artistic merit from moral tendency.

Griswold's succeeding Poe is perhaps a sufficient explanation of why Mrs. Sigourney sent no more verses to *Graham's* in 1842, and why, a year later, she was surprised to receive a request for contributions. How could Griswold address her after that insolent paragraph? What sort of man was he? She wrote cautiously to Mrs. Stephens, who had worked with Griswold after Poe's abrupt departure. The impulsive reply of this loquacious lady throws valuable light on the Evil Angel to whom Poe was soon to intrust his literary remains:

. . . I *do* know the Rev R Griswold. Your opinion was correct he is a man of talent and poetical research but you ask my opinion in confidence and in confidence I give it—he is a man constitutionally incapable of speaking the truth, a sycophant in your company, a serpent in the company of those who like to hear you unjustly spoken of—a man incapable of steady friendship or enmity, in short a moral coward and a dangerous person to be connected with. But he is a useful Editor and invaluable to Mr Graham from his industry taste and above all from his soft manner and cringing habits which make him remarkably popular with a certain class of writers. Whatever he has said of you has been said fifty times of every writer in the country, and if he has given an unfavorable opinion one day be assured a favorable one was given the next. His conduct toward myself was utterly unprincipled and nothing but my personal influence with Mr Graham, which happened to be more powerful than he dreamed of, prevented him doing me a serious injury. When he saw that any further attempt to wrong me would be likely to ruin himself he became humble enough and the second time I ever saw him in my life he completely astonished me by the humility of his apologies, apologies that would have been more valuable if they had seemed to cost any sacrifice of pride to principle.

I have not a particle of ill feeling toward Mr Griswold, in truth it seems to me that he ought to be incapable of creating strong feelings of any kind; his want of truth justice and dignity seems to be an infirmity rather than a vice. He is said to have been a kind husband and father—Now, I am told, the

death of his wife has caused a change for the better in his
character, he seemed completely broken hearted when I saw
him in Philadelphia last March. I may be prejudiced in my
opinion but it *is* my opinion, which, however, I would not speak
or write except as you have desired it and as you may require a
knowledge of the man in your connection with the magazine.
Write nothing to him which may not be exhibited. Whatever
confidential business you have do it with Mr Graham, and rest
assured that any opinion he may give of you or your literary
character will never find a listener where he is known. Even
though you were not known: If Mr G can travel so far as the
place where his word would effect a reputation like yours he
may hope to immortalize [?] himself in some way. Do not
think me unjustly severe I could not write frankly and write
otherwise, harsh as it may seem.[272]

Despite the acrimonious intrigues of the *literati* and
daily demands for contributions to the periodicals, Mrs.
Sigourney found time between 1840 and 1850 to publish
fourteen volumes. The first important one was *Pocahontas,* which appeared in 1841, in London before her departure, and in America soon after her return home. For
several years she had been considering another poem on
the Indians. They had been pushed farther west, but her
sympathy followed them, and in 1839 she was writing the
member of Congress from Wisconsin territory, urging
measures to admit them to citizenship, and offering gifts
of her books.[273] She was not satisfied with the Pocahontas
episode in *Traits of the Aborigines;* could she not write a
poem that would treat it with more color and passion?
Not passion as one saw it among the lower orders, to be
sure, but such chaste passion as the first Christian Indian must have felt. Alexander Everett, whom she consulted, agreed that Pocahontas was probably the finest

subject for poetry that the whole history of the world
could furnish; but he suggested that a work of any
length on a historical theme, he would rather incline to
write as a novel, ''the true Epic of modern times.'' In
prose she would be able to introduce a few comic scenes,
such as the auctioning of the wives at Jamestown. Prose,
too, would solve another problem: what to use in place of
the name *Smith,* which Mrs. Sigourney quite rightly felt
''would be inadmissable in verse.'' If she wished to make
it poetic, Scott and Byron were the best models; still ''it
would be rather dangerous,'' he added, ''to follow closely
in the track of either.''[274]

The poem never reached epic proportions. In its final
form it consists of fifty-four pseudo-Spenserian stanzas
that follow Mrs. Hemans' *Forest Sanctuary* rather than
The Faerie Queene or *Childe Harold,* introducing a
rhymed couplet for the fifth and sixth lines and an additional rhyme for the final couplet. That Scott was not altogether neglected, however, one may judge by compar-
ing the first line of the poem,

> Clime of the West! that, slumbering long and deep

with

> Harp of the North! that moldering long has hung,

the beginning of *The Lady of the Lake.* Lines of a de-
cidedly Byronic cast were quoted in the last chapter.
There are indications that Mrs. Sigourney made an effort
to restrain her ''overgemmy'' style; but though the language is sometimes less stilted, the characters portrayed
are the stock figures of the religious annuals. The narrative, if it may be so called, begins with the landing of the
Jamestown settlers in 1607. By the ninth stanza Mrs. Sig-

ourney slides easily into the old formula. The daring cavaliers sent out by the London Company are merely the old puppets, the religious pioneers.

> Yet, mid their cares, one hallow'd dome they rear'd,
> To nurse devotion's consecrated flame.[275]

Their labors and adventures in the new country are passed over in silence for a seven-stanza description of the "Sabbath morn."

> Here, in his surplice white, the pastor stood,
> A holy man, of countenance serene[276]

—the very same figure, indeed, who officiated at *The Sailor's Funeral,* and at every wedding and christening Mrs. Sigourney ever wrote about.

The dramatic scene where Pocahontas saves Captain Smith is given with more restraint than in *Traits of the Aborigines,* but it fails to move us.

> The sentenced captive see—his brow how white!
> Stretch'd on the turf his manly form lies low,
> The war-club poises for its fatal blow,
>   The death-mist swims before his darken'd sight:
>   Forth springs the child, in tearful pity bold,
> Her head on his declines, her arms his neck enfold.[277]

> Know'st thou what thou hast done, thou dark-hair'd child?

inquires the bard; and in true form, answers her own question:

> As little knew the princess who descried
> A floating speck on Egypt's turbid tide,
>   A bulrush-ark the matted reeds among,
>   And, yielding to an infant's tearful smile,
> Drew forth Jehovah's seer, from the devouring Nile.[278]

The next dramatic occurrence is the baptism of the Indian maid:

> The Triune Name is breathed with hallow'd power,
> The dew baptismal bathes the forest-flower.[279]

Then Romance enters her life. Until her conversion, "nature's fervent child" had been entirely without knowledge of love, which, it seems, civilization alone can bestow. For

> love to her pure breast was but a name
> For kindling knowledge, and for taste refined,
> A guiding lamp, whose bright, mysterious flame
> Led on to loftier heights the aspiring mind.[280]

But this is as near passion as Mrs. Sigourney ever dared come. One of the world's most romantic courtships is ignored; and Pocahontas sits studying sacred history until the next stanza brings one abruptly to her wedding.

Only familiarity with the story tells the reader that she is marrying Rolfe, and not John Smith, neither of whom is named. The young bridegroom stands in the church, hailing the red men as brothers,

> While the old white-hair'd king, with eye of pride,
> Gives to his ardent hand the timid, trusting bride,[281]

who has certainly lost all the daring with which she confronted the executioners' uplifted clubs.

The picture of the young wife is another of the "gemmy," ideal conceptions. Like all Mrs. Sigourney's characters, Pocahontas is simply an abstraction of Virtue; and except for variations in the color of their hair, and the fact that one "towers" while the other

"shrinks," it is almost impossible to tell the young lady
from her father. But they are soon to part. Pocahontas
follows her husband to England, or rather "Albion."
Here "mid the gorgeous domes of ancient days," or
"mid the magic of those regal walls,"

> Stole back the scenery of her solitude:
> An aged father, in his cabin rude,
>   Mix'd with her dreams a melancholy moan,
> Notching his simple calendar with pain,
> And straining his red eye to watch the misty main[282]

for a daughter who will return to him nevermore.

As might be expected the poem reaches its climax with
Pocahontas' death. A rather lengthy farewell address to
her grieving husband is still unfinished when

> with a marble coldness on her cheek,
> And one long moan, like breathing harp-string sweet,
> She bare the unspoken lore to her Redeemer's feet.[283]

But the end is not yet. It was a trick of the "graveyard"
school of poets to revive the dead whenever it could be
contrived. In this instance it is found that Pocahontas'
infant son had missed the final leavetaking.

> Lo! in his nurse's arms he careless came,
> A noble creature, with his full dark eye
> And clustering curls, in nature's majesty;
>   But, with a sudden shriek, his mother's name
> Burst from his lips, and, gazing on the clay,
> He stretch'd his eager arms where the cold sleeper lay.

> "Oh mother! mother!" Did that bitter cry
>   Send a shrill echo through the realm of death?
> Look, to the trembling fringes of the eye.
>   List, the sharp shudder of returning breath,

> The spirit's sob! They lay him on her breast;
> One long, long kiss on his bright brow she press'd;
> Even from heaven's gate of bliss she lingereth,
> To breathe one blessing o'er his precious head,
> And then her arm unclasps, and she is of the dead.[284]

Griswold, who was not a gentle critic, regarded this as the best of Mrs. Sigourney's long poems, and "much the best of the many poetical compositions of which the famous daughter of Powhatan has been the subject."[285] But it has stood the test of time as badly as all her others.

In 1842, besides *Pleasant Memories,* Mrs. Sigourney published in Philadelphia a volume called *Poems,* that was composed largely of verses from her earlier books, a good third of them being lifted from the 1834 *Poems,* and arranged in different order, with some judicious changes of titles by which, for example, *The Death of a Missionary to Liberia* becomes *The Death of a Missionary in Africa.* The year 1843 saw no new book; but a second edition of *Pleasant Memories* that was called for emboldened the publishers, Munroe & Company of Boston, to accept a companion work called *Scenes in My Native Land,* which was to consist of prose and verse descriptions of notable places in America. As Mrs. Sigourney could not visit all of them personally, she drew freely on the descriptions of other writers. Accompanied by Andrew, she did go again to Niagara in June, 1844, to deepen her impression of nine years before. Like a true sentimentalist, she viewed the falls chiefly through their effect on this tall, silent lad of fourteen, who escaped when he could to meditate alone, free from the maternal probings after his thoughts. Her first visit there had been made with Mr. and Mrs. Griffin of Staten Island.[286] Mr. Griffin, during her early years as a writer, had arranged many of her contracts with publishers; but ten years of authorship and household economy had taught her much, and her correspondence shows that she was now quite able to hold her own in business affairs.

The second edition of *Pleasant Memories* had not sold well, the copies Mrs. Sigourney purchased for gifts having more than absorbed her royalties. If Munroe & Company really wanted her new book, she wrote them, they would have to pay more for it.

It is necessary for one, whose subsistence is derived from the pen, not to devote the principal portion of time to the composition of consecutive works, but to articles for periodicals, which give a reasonable degree of profit. . . . I cannot do justice to myself, to compose a work of this nature (and which I have no doubt will be saleable) for less than 15 cents per copy, on an edition of 2000, one half to be paid (as I have been accustomed to receive it) on the reception of the manuscript, and the remainder, in six months, or a year after publication.[287]

The Munroes accepted this 50 per cent increase with good grace; but they soon had reason to regret it, for *Scenes in My Native Land* proved a failure. The American public was not interested in reading secondhand impressions of familiar places, even in blank verse, though in England, for the same reason, the book sold better than *Pleasant Memories*. Realizing that she had overstepped, Mrs. Sigourney wrote the publishers that the low state of her health had perhaps affected the quality of *Scenes*, and generously renounced her claim to the second payment, except on volumes actually sold.[288]

Most of the other books that appeared between 1840 and 1850 were recombinations of earlier works. A whole edition of *Poetry for Seamen* (1845), which contained all the poems Mrs. Sigourney had written about ships and sailors, with a generous addition of temperance hymns, was given by a philanthropic gentleman[289] for distribution at a Boston Mission. *The Voice of Flowers* (1846) gathered into a popular little 32mo all her poems about flowers, while *The Weeping Willow* (1847) collected no less than seventy obituary poems into 128 pages. *Myrtis* (1846) consisted of historical tales, and *Water-Drops* (1848), poems and stories of temperance. During these years there were also new editions of such old favorites as *Letters to Mothers, Letters to Young Ladies,* and *Select Poems;*[290] and even the *Religious Souvenirs* were reissued as *The Religious Keepsake* from the ten-year-old plates. Her name alone could sell them. Her popularity was at its height.

Recognition came with the proposal of the Philadelphia publishers, Carey & Hart, to bring out an illustrated edition of her poems, uniform with those they had already issued of Bryant, Longfellow, and Willis. These three poets were acknowledged immortals, and to appear in their company with the same gilt edges and morocco was a sort of assumption. "I was not insensible to so high a compliment," says Mrs. Sigourney with her characteristic understatement, "and acceded to their wishes."[291] The book was to be a large octavo of more than four hundred pages with fourteen engravings from designs of the celebrated illustrator, F. O. C. Darley, and for the frontispiece an engraving of the fair authoress herself.

Now all previous portraits of the lady had failed to please those exacting friends of hers; daguerreotypes, which had lately appeared, were even less satisfactory. But there was a miniature painted in 1841 or 1842[292] that represented her as she might have looked at the time of her marriage. The slim figure, the girlish face, the eyes

large, but soft under prettily arched brows, the slender
neck, and, above all, the most daintily tapering hands—
self-consciously displayed against the dark background—
pleased both the sitter and her friends.

In 1848, when she sent this "likeness" to Philadelphia
to be engraved by Cheney for the new work, she wrote
that it was painted "three summers since";[293] and so by
simple arithmetic that puzzling measure of time, the
summer, is found to be exactly two years. The artist had
always objected to having it engraved for fear it would
be injured; and now to make doubly sure that no harm
would come to this "expensive work of art," Mrs. Sigourney had Mary add to the letter a little note in her own
hand:

I hope the greatest care may be used, in regard to the accompanying miniature. It is the only correct likeness of her,
which has ever been taken, and as it is intended for me, I feel
some solicitude concerning it. Should any injury befal it, it
can never be replaced and I therefore trust you will excuse my
anxiety.[294]

Occasionally, during the six months the precious picture
was away, little postscripts were added to her letters:
"My daughter bids me ask when she may have her treas-
ured miniature again."[295] As the time for the appearance
of the great volume drew near, Mrs. Sigourney's excitement increased. Again and again she reminds the publishers that "it is of some consequence to me and my
friends, to have a good likeness, inasmuch as all previous
ones have been unsatisfactory. Will it be of any use for
me to come to Philadelphia a few days, either on that account or to expedite the progress of the proofs. . . ?"[296]

Daniel Wadsworth, to whom she planned to dedicate
the book, died in the summer of 1848. Three weeks later

she wrote Carey & Hart: "Please to mention in your next, whether in your opinion, a dedication to the venerable poet, Rogers, of London, will be an advantage to the book in any way, or the reverse."[297] Having received their assurance that it would add considerable éclat, she wrote the following:

TO SAMUEL ROGERS
THE MOST VENERABLE POET OF EUROPE,
AND THE FRIEND OF AMERICA,
WHOSE STRAINS, READ IN THE SOLITUDE OF EARLY YEARS,
AND WHOSE KIND WORDS TO THE STRANGER IN HIS OWN HOME,
ARE ALIKE HELD AMONG THE
"PLEASURES OF MEMORY,"
THIS VOLUME IS RESPECTFULLY INSCRIBED.[298]

The "banker-poet" was eighty-five years old, and sufficiently experienced to realize how Mrs. Sigourney's tribute had come his way; but, debonair to the last, he wrote:

My DEAR Mʳˢ SIGOURNEY

What can I say—What return can I make for the Honour you propose to me, an Honour so undeserved?—Yet undeserved as it is, I cannot say *No* & whatever may happen, I shall always feel the prouder for it so long as I live. The Atlantic is no Obstacle to your rendering a Service.

Has it never been your Intention to come & see us again? Pray come as soon as you *can* & when you have seen the Sisterhood at Hampstead (for the Ladies* are still by their fireside & were yesterday enquiring after you with a warmth that would have gone to your heart) pray, pray descend to a small door in a dark & narrow street, a street in a City where there are at least two millions of People. It will fly open at your Ap-

---

* Joanna Baillie and her sister Agnes.

proach if He is still to be found there—but dont be long for his lease is a very short one.

Yours ever most sincerely

SAMUEL ROGERS . . .[299]

When the heavy volume with polished edges and elaborately tooled turkey morocco ($7 in leather, $5 in cloth) stood on Mrs. Sigourney's table between *Longfellow* and *Bryant,* she felt that at last there was no disputing her place in the nation's literature. Here was material proof of her rank among the great poets of the time. She ruffled the tissue paper that protected the frontispiece and gazed critically at the miniature. It had lost none of its porcelain prettiness in the engraving, and it stared back at her with the fixed and startled animation that had aroused Mrs. Carlyle's venom. Lifting her eyes unconsciously to the mirror above the table, she was shocked by the contrast—the deep lines about the mouth, the sagging chin, and dull, gray hair showing beneath the still-glossy ringlets. Her next birthday would be the sixtieth. Why had she felt so indignant when the milliner in fitting her hat that morning had remarked that it was a becoming fashion for an *old lady?*[300] After all, what was so frightful about that little word *old?* It was only with age that one became "venerable." Perhaps the time had come to yield.

In Washington a few months later she went with Mary to hear Webster arguing an important case before the Supreme Court. Donald Grant Mitchell, who was in the audience, records the appearance of the "modest Connecticut mistress of the crafts of poesy" in *American Lands and Letters:*[301]

. . . [Mrs. Sigourney] came with a young friend, at a late hour, when the old cavernous recesses of the Court were nearly

filled with eager attendants. Mr. Webster, rolling his great
eyes around the chamber, as was his wont—noticed the late
arrival of the poetess, and rising—left his briefs—strode up
the crowded alley-way, and greeting her in his largest manner, insisted upon escorting her—as if she were a queen, and
he, master of royal ceremonies—down to the very front of the
Chamber, where he found her a place among the distinguished
advocates. The old lady bore the unusual and marked attention
with a little nervous trepidation, yet with a glow of gratification that lighted beamingly her fine matronly face. I think she
never felt more touched by any public recognition of her literary or social consequence.

The sun had not shone in Hartford that day; and by
evening the damp, biting wind that whistled up Main
Street had driven indoors all but a few shivering apprentices, who were putting shutters on the shop windows.
Somewhat stooping and more deliberate in his gait, but
punctual as ever, Mr. Sigourney wrapped his blue camlet
cloak closer about him as he left the hardware store.

CHAPTER SIX

THE FADED HOPE

"I BEG you will excuse the chirography of some of the
manuscript that comes to you by this Express,"
Mrs. Sigourney wrote her publisher in 1848, when
the press of the holiday season had compelled her "to use
the services of a young amanuensis or two, who do not
write as plainly as I could wish."[302] One may easily imagine that before the letter was posted it served as a gentle reproof to the young offenders, Mary and Andrew.
They were reaching an age at which their mother's
meticulous system of education was beginning to lose its
hold, and she was often shocked to hear them voice opinions quite different from her own. This variation of their
handwriting from her careful copperplate model was
only a symptom of far deeper spiritual changes. They
were displaying the first faint stirrings of forces that
were soon with much struggle and bitterness to assail the
Practical Ideal in American life.

Like most children of the time the Sigourneys had been
brought up on the fundamentally Hebraic conception
that to love God and serve him was the sure way to
wealth and happiness. The Reverend Joel Hawes, pastor
of the Congregational church, whose sermons their
mother used frequently to hear, was a champion of this

principle; and his *Lectures to Young Men* repeat again and again in forceful italics that "regard to duty, is the surest way to *promote one's temporal interests*,"[303] and that reputation is worth more to a man than the richest capital because *"it makes friends; it creates funds; it draws around him patronage and support; and opens for him a sure and easy way to wealth, to honor and happiness."*[304] "If there were nothing beyond the grave," the same book adds, "and no motive for keeping the Sabbath, but your prosperity in this life, you would be unspeakable losers not to keep it. No habitual Sabbath breaker can be permanently prosperous."[305] The thought is punctuated by the remark of a man "of very high standing," "that those merchants in New-York, who have kept their counting rooms open on the Sabbath, during my residence there (twenty-five years), have failed, without an exception."[306]

During the first half of the nineteenth century the Practical Ideal, this austere combination of Puritanism with the philosophy of Poor Richard, held sway unchallenged; and according to many thoughtful observers it is still the most powerful influence in American life. It was taught at home, from the pulpit, and in the schoolroom. Both boys and girls were given to read little Juvenile Guides in which righteousness was urged through contemplation of the evil ends to which transgressors always came; and from these faded, but unthumbed volumes, it is possible to picture, if not what American children really were, at least what their elders wanted them to be.

Above all other virtues the Practical Ideal set obedience. To be called a "law-abiding" citizen was to be highly complimented. Uppermost in the moralist's mind was the proverb: "He that keepeth the law, happy is

Wood Engraving from
"Tommy Wellwood"

One of the Juvenile Publications of
The American Tract Society.

he." And naturally his children were taught first of all obedience, instant and unquestioning—obedience to God's will, found literally in the Bible, and to that of his earthly representative, the head of the household, who was just a little lower than the angels. The father's will was law to which both wife and children bowed; all the juvenile literature of the period attests the extent of his power. Cousin Lucy, for example, little Rollo's female counterpart, takes cold, and the doctor is called to see her. " 'Will she take *ipecacuanha?*' said the doctor to Lucy's mother. 'She will take anything you prescribe, doctor,' said her father, in reply.' '[307] The mother, it will be noticed, to whom the question was addressed, is given no chance to answer; and father's firm tone leaves little doubt that Lucy, who is the soul of propriety, will do exactly as she is told.

Indeed, much of life was ipecacuanha to these little people; but God had ordained it so, and he who would be rich and happy, would swallow it without wry faces. To begin with there was that distasteful business of early rising. "Every boy who means to be useful, good, or happy, should learn to rise early in the morning," declares the first sentence in William A. Alcott's *Boy's Guide to Usefulness.*[308] Though few ten-year-old boys aspire to be centenarians, a great list is given of eminent men with ages to one hundred and over, whose longevity is attributed solely to their rising at four in winter and three in summer. No time gained by retiring later in the evening can ever take the place of those virtuous cold gray hours between four and six.

Should any one wish to know why this is so [the *Guide* continues], I can only say that, to give him the reasons in full, would lead us quite away, into the regions both of physics and metaphysics; and that, for the present, I believe he must try to content himself with the mere assertion that it is so. . . . Such, I say again, is the constitution of things, as established by Him who made both the evening and the morning; and who made the one for sleep, and the other for action.[309]

And, as if the list of old men were not enough, he adds a sonorous roster of famous early risers, beginning with Abraham, Moses, David, Solomon, and Paul, and ending with Napoleon and Wellington![310]

Content perforce with this psychology, the good child, tumbling out of bed at, say, four o'clock, performed what were known as "ablutions." *The Boy's Guide* suggests a number of painful processes to add to the terror of icy water, chief among which is a violent friction with a pair of coarse mittens. Now that he was up, he could spend some time in "self-examination and prayer."

You may sing, if you please; for singing will help to make you feel more disposed for prayer. . . . If any boy ten years old, or even no more than seven, who has been taught to read and think, can be found destitute of devotional feelings when he first rises in the morning, especially if he rises early,—for the morning is certainly the best time of the day for devotion, —I know not what should be thought of him. He must certainly be very strangely constituted.[311]

At the table he was told to "accept of what is given you, asking no questions and making no complaints."[312] He was particularly cautioned against eating too much, and the lesson was enforced with a horrid story of a boy who, being fond of fruit, "became habitually a glutton, and . . . died when little more than thirty years of age."[313] Talking and laughing at table, aside from their impropriety, were forbidden as dangerous, for particles of food might lodge in the windpipe. To impress this:

Surgeons, indeed, sometimes cut open this pipe,—which can easily be come at, in the forepart of the throat,—and take out the substance which had fallen in, and thus save the person's life; though even this severe measure will not always save life; for I have known some children die after they have submitted to the operation.[314]

"I have taken for granted that you love labor," the *Guide* says;[315] but to make his abhorrence of idleness evident, he relates an anecdote to show the terrible effects of this evil. The indolent boys, at first lazy, soon become vicious; "for Satan, finding them unemployed, provided them with work enough. They could very soon rob birds' nests, chew tobacco, smoke, use bad language, drink rum, quarrel, and even defraud and steal,"[316] in several of which accomplishments many of the *Guide's* readers must have envied them, in spite of their having had to quit the country and coming to bad ends. Work in the garden was generally recommended as an amusing exercise; but any sort of work was preferable to idleness. The *Guide* tells with approval of

one father who used to require it of his sons to spend a certain number of hours every day in piling up stones, though he had no further use for them, after they were piled up, than to have them taken down and piled up again in another place.[317]

Having followed the *Guide* thus far, one is not surprised by the query, "Is it right to play?"[318] To decide this question Alcott calls in the authority of both the Old and New Testaments, concluding ponderously: "Let it stand, then, as an indisputable fact, that it is right to play, . . ."[319] but only at the right times, gently, coolly,

and with *good* companions. "Remember God sees you,"
he warns them. "Some boys seem to me to forget, wholly,
that God sees them while at play . . .";[320] for whom he
recommends a chapter in Ecclesiastes that will remind
them the day is coming when they must answer even for
the way they have played. Shuttlecock, ninepins, quoits,
and ball are acceptable games; but leapfrog is "coarse"
and swimming dangerous. Dancing is to be avoided because of the temptations with which it is fraught as well
as the chance of taking a chill. People who dance eventually catch a hard cold; then rheumatism sets in, followed by "fever, or consumption, and finally decline and
death."[321]

The Puritan conscience was satisfied only with useful
amusements. Theaters, puppet shows, and circuses were
alike forbidden; card playing was "immoral." Military
parades were injurious, according to one writer, because
they leave the mind "with nothing satisfactory, instruc-
tive or useful, to fix upon," though "the annual exhibi-
tions of Infant and Sabbath schools, if properly con-
ducted, will afford a source of rational entertainment to
the young."[322] The only toys that were tolerated on Sunday were those like Noah's ark that would serve as illustrations for the Scripture lesson; and for week days,
spades, rakes, and hoes would do most toward interesting
the young in the Practical Ideal.

Similar influences hedged in a boy's reading. For the
normal lad of fifteen the *Guide* suggests biographies—the
lives of Oberlin, Hannah More, and the apostle John;
but they must be biographies of *excellent* people. "For
example, read the lives of Paul, and Howard, and Wil-
berforce, and Washington, rather than those of Alexander, Charles XII., and Napoleon Bonaparte. The less

boys and young men know of such men as these last, the better. . . ."[323] Fictitious works were to be avoided. This attitude was not, however, limited to America, for even so intelligent a man as Dr. Thomas Arnold decried the effect of novels, ascribing what seemed to him the growing fault of childishness in boys "to the great number of exciting books of amusement like Pickwick and Nickleby,"[324] works which the modern schoolmaster cannot force upon his pupils. *The Boy's Guide* frowns even on *Robinson Crusoe:* "Robinson Crusoe has a charm for many minds, and yet I do not like it. I have seldom known a boy made better or more contented by it; if, indeed, it made him any wiser. I wish to have no friends of mine ever read Robinson Crusoe."[325]

But there was one book every child was expected to keep well thumbed—"that pure and infallible source of instruction,"[326] the Bible. The accepted age for beginning its study was three years,[327] though if a child were capable of understanding earlier, it should not be postponed. The parent, too, says Mrs. Sigourney's friend, Theodore Dwight, Jr., in *The Father's Book,* must study the Bible daily himself,

often alluding to what he has read . . . and occasionally repeating with fervor, in the presence of his children, passages appropriate to the circumstances in which he is placed. . . . The Bible should always be presented as the book of the highest value in every respect, and connected with every department of education. Guard, carefully guard your children from imbibing any idea of its inferiority to what are called classical books, in wisdom, taste or refinement. . . .[328] Let it always be at hand, always treated with reverence in conduct and conversation, appealed to in every case of doubt, and made the standard for our own opinions, thoughts, principles and actions.[329]

For the child, Bible study is, of course, a daily task; but on Sunday—on the Sabbath—the little, worn volume scarcely leaves his hand. When he has finished his private devotions, he takes it with him to his father's room.

Experience has taught him that his father's brow is peculiarly serene, on a Sabbath morning. . . .

"My dear child," the father may say, "how kind God is to give us another Sabbath day! Here we are, all well, with a house to live in, and many good things around us, no noise to disturb us, and the Bible to learn out of! . . . I have thanked God once this morning; but I love to thank Him and pray to Him with my child. . . . Come, let us kneel down."

Perhaps the child will express reluctance, or be attracted by something he sees through the window. . . .[330]

But that is unlikely if he is more than three years old.

The father now opens the Bible: or the child, if he has been accustomed to this kind of treatment, will probably say: "Dear father, shall I get you the Bible?"[331]

And so the lesson begins.

The aim of such an education was not to make the child happier in this world; indeed, these pious people were not altogether sure that it was right to be happy in this world. The process was rather to fit children for a better world, to prepare them for immortality. "You are now to lay your course for eternity," proclaimed Dr. Hawes; "to enter upon that path which, in all probability, you will pursue through life, and which will terminate in heaven or in hell."[332] By such counsel the young minds were directed toward death and the glorious scenes to which it would introduce them. The most shocking "thriller" of today is less harrowing than the children's tales published by the American Tract Society to further juvenile meditations on this theme. Tommy Well-wood, for instance, the son of a Scotch clergyman, is sent to grammar school, where, at first, he trembled "to see the evil tricks, and hear the horrid tongues of his little school-fellows,"[333] but later lost his piety and became bold himself. He is soon summoned home by the death of his mother, most minutely described, who bequeaths him her Bible and blessing.

The day of the funeral, and next day, he read a good deal, not without tears, in his mother's dear legacy. But the day after that, the habits of the little grammar school infidel began to return, and he went out with Cesar [the Newfoundland dog] without saying any prayers, or reading any of the holy book. Mary [his sister] had gone out with her Bible in her hand, and was sitting reading by the morning sun, on a *gowany* bank beside the little brook that gurgled down the *brae* to the river —"Remember now thy Creator in the days of thy youth," &c.

Tommy came by, and began to play in the brook, but would not read with his sister, and talked some naughty words.

Mary. O, Tommy! speak not so. I fear you are forgetting to be good, for you did not say your prayers this morning, and you won't read God's word with me.

Tommy. I am as good as you, sister Mary, though I am not always reading my Bible, and praying like you.

Mary. But, oh! Tommy, should you die, and be carried away in a coffin like mamma, what would become of you then?

Tommy. Eh! what did you say? Poor mamma! (and he burst into tears)—I would go up yonder where mamma is, if I died —and he looked up to the blue heavens.

Mary, tears blinding her eyes, turns over the leaves of her Bible without seeing them, stops "at a place she had often read: Matt, chap. xxv. 31," and begins to lecture Tommy on the Last Judgment.

Mamma said, the sheep are the righteous, and the goats are the wicked. . . . Oh! do you not remember the hymn,

"There is a dreadful hell,
"And everlasting pains:
"There sinners must with devils dwell,
"In darkness, fire, and chains."

Tommy drew near and sat down beside his sister.—What then must we do to be saved, Mary?

She tells him in a manner Jonathan Edwards would have admired, and, converted, he promises to be good.

> *Tommy.* I will—I will—let us go to my mother's grave—And off he ran . . . to tell mamma the new resolution of his soul. Mary followed after, pensively and slowly, with her open Bible pressed to her little beating heart.[334]

Mrs. Sigourney herself wrote often in this pious vein; but in bringing up her children she was not quite so rigorous. Though she had read *Robinson Crusoe* at the age of four without feeling hurt by it,[335] the books Andrew noted in his diary are of a very moral character. He read the Psalms aloud to his grandfather;[336] he memorized hymns by the hundred to recite to his mother on Sundays;[337] and besides her *Biographies of Pious Persons*,[338] his reading list included such works as the lives of Pastor Oberlin[339] and President Edwards,[340] *Doddridge's Rise and Progress of Religion*,[341] Mrs. Hooker's *Biographies of the Prophets*,[342] and *Pilgrim's Progress*[343] —all before he was ten years old. The morality that permeates his diary was, of course, absorbed from his mother, who seems to have dictated much of it. For example:

This is my birth-day. Now, I am a boy seven years old. May God please to make me better than I ever was before. My goodness is but a poor little weak leaf. Yet I hope it will grow to be a bud, and a flower; and to bear fruit in heaven.

Or such an observation as this:

Yesterday, I saw a horse turning a wheel to help print Bibles. I thought he was doing a very good work for a horse.[344]

She must also have been responsible for his mild version of the "Rape of the Sabine Women," who display real Christian piety in persuading the "frowning" Romans to shake hands with their husbands instead of fighting. "All women should try to be peace-makers,"[345] wrote Andrew. There is no question that he learned from his mother the didactic habit that led him to address his moral remarks to an imaginary Sunday-school class. "My child-reader," says he, " 'remember Thy Creator . . .' " Or again, "I hope that all of you, children, will be Christians."[346] He was eight when he informed them that as men "we can row a boat, or steer a large vessel, or be a minister, or a shoe maker. All are useful,—but I advise you to be a minister. . . ."[347] And his mother smiled to see how tractable the young mind was. He took the temperance pledge the next year. "During vacations," his mother wrote in her most execrable style, "he felt it a duty to inquire into the component parts of whatever questionable condiment solicited his taste, and if the pudding-sauce had admitted an infusion of wine among its elements, could only satisfy his conscience, by quitting the table."[348]

Among the boys of the neighborhood such consistent piety was not impressive. Andrew was small for his years, quite unprepossessing in manner, and by turns either morbidly diffident or inclined to lecture rather priggishly. Besides, he had inherited from his father a

most un-boylike sense of precision. Everything he owned
had its exact place. ''Who has moved that book, two
inches further to the northwest?''[349] his mother heard
him ask one day. Ordinary lads did not comprehend such
refinements; they thought Andrew a ''sissy'' and let him
alone.

His personality had its first chance to emerge from the
maternal influence when Mrs. Sigourney went abroad in
1840, leaving him in a boarding school. In the beginning
the boys had little to do with him, for he was smaller than
most of them and afraid to join in their games; but during the presidential campaign of that year Andrew made
a stirring speech in favor of General Harrison, perched
on the roof of a log cabin the older lads had built, and
from then on he began to make a few friends. All his life
he had accepted opinions from his mother; now he began
to form some of his own. Her first shock on her return
was to find that the boy in whom her fondness had so
easily discerned the poetic temperament had come to consider the writing of verses effeminate. Still worse, the
naïve confidence with which he had poured out all his
thoughts to her had vanished.

By the time he was fourteen a settled taciturnity baf-
fled her every effort to follow the working of his mind. In
spite of her careful nurture, he was becoming like his father, close, cool, deliberate, not toward her alone, but
even with friends of his own age. In his diary he wrote a
code of ''PRIVATE AND PRACTICAL LAWS TO BE
COMMITTED TO MEMORY, AND ALWAYS OB-
SERVED IN THE REGULATION OF LIFE,'' among
which one finds such cautious precepts as these:

Closely observe, and carefully inquire into all the points of
character of one who wishes to become my friend.

Never venture to make predictions, without full acquaintance with all the premises on which a prediction should rest.

Learn the best method of turning to account everything that I may possess.

Keep my own secrets. What you keep yourself, you know is kept: what is in the keeping of others, you cannot be sure of.[350]

One of the few extant letters in Andrew's handwriting is a curious example of the practical application of his code:

Mr. William R. Lawrence will please to keep for Sale, the bowie-knife delivered to him by A. M. Sigourney, present owner. He will please keep it in the *same condition* as delivered to him by the owner, and endeavor, by *activity & perseverance,* to sell the above knife *at or before Thursday, April 19th., 1849,* at 8 P.M. The price of knife $2.00, (if possible,) & no less than, $1.75, *as the lowest price.* The proceeds of Sale to be received by Mr. Lawrence, *at the instant of selling, & paid in specie.* Mr. W. R. L. will please call on A. M. Sigourney, at 8 P.M. of *next Thursday, April 19th.,* & deliver the proceeds of this Sale.

Signed,

A. M. B. Sigourney.

Apr. 18th., '49.[351]

It seems incredible that a boy of eighteen who had spent nearly a year in college could have written such a document seriously to his best friend. Yet Charles J. Hoadley, state librarian of Connecticut, who knew the family well and was Mrs. Sigourney's literary executor, wrote at the bottom of it: ''This note is very characteristic of Andrew Sigourney.''

With such a personality, it would be surprising to find that his experience at Trinity College had been altogether agreeable. One day toward the end of the first year he came home and announced with his customary precision that, having considered the matter carefully, he was going to become a soldier. Mrs. Sigourney was stunned by the news. For a quarter of a century she had written in behalf of peace. Andrew himself had copied for her the story of Frank Ludlow, who had disobeyed his mother's dying injunction and gone off to fight in the War of 1812. Like all disobedient sons, Frank Ludlow came to a bad end, deserting three times to see his wife and children, and being shot just as his good brother Edward, the clergyman, arrived to read the burial service. Frank's last words were: "O mother! mother! had I but believed—."[352] But Andrew had lived behind the scenes with these puppets too long to be suitably impressed. He had a healthy dislike for the priggish Edward, who as a child preferred Antoninus Pius ("He reigned 22 years, and died with many friends, surrounding his bed, at the age of 74")[353] to Frank's hero, Charles XII of Sweden. The army would offer some excitement, a change of surroundings, as well as a chance of eluding an overvigilant mother's scrutiny. Couldn't some of her influential friends help him get into West Point?

Mrs. Sigourney was wondering who had suggested the hideous idea to her only son. Was it perverse stubbornness that made him choose the warrior's career? Tearful entreaty failed to swerve him; and when the unpleasant reality seemed inevitable, the sentimentalist in her found another explanation: It was the "voice of the old soldier, mingling with his cradle-dream, tales of Washington, and the times that tried men's souls."[354] He was taking after that blessed patriot, her father. Reluctantly, she promised to apply for the appointment.

Meanwhile Andrew began a course of Spartan exercise to inure himself to the field of battle. The long solitary walks of which he had always been fond were extended until they reached a length of twenty or thirty miles. Proper protection from the cold was rejected as effeminate, and the fatigue and lassitude that assailed him after these exertions he determined to root out through ascetic discipline and diet. At last one day in June, 1849, his mother laid before him on the table a thick file of correspondence. There were letters from two successive Presidents, the member of Congress from Hartford, a Justice of the Supreme Court, an Attorney General, and even one—a very kind and intimate one—from old Mrs. Dolly Madison,[355] who had interceded with the Secretary of War. But the application for admission to the Academy had come too late.

"Is there no longer any hope?" he asked, and being assured there was not, declined to read the carefully arranged letters. Even the flattering compliments of Mrs. Madison could not pique his curiosity. A slight paling of the lip as he drew it firm was the only sign his mother observed of the pang the disappointment caused him.[356]

In this matter the Lord seemed to have answered her prayers. But there was another instance in which her supplication had been more prolonged and less successful —the conversion of her children. Mrs. Sigourney had been brought up in uncompromising New England Calvinism. At the time of her marriage, when she began to attend the Episcopal church, she brought with her a more rigid interpretation of the Thirty-Nine Articles than most of her fellow parishioners would have thought necessary. Her children were instructed from the tenderest age in religious doctrine, and the earnest little faces, upturned to heaven as they said their evening prayers, seemed to assure the anxious mother that they indeed were of the elect. As they grew older, however, the chasm that yawns between all but the wisest parents and their children gaped wide. They did not feel the need for an experience of conversion. In spite of her scrupulous training they were nearly as unregenerate as heathen. Mary could not be persuaded by prayer or argument until at length, quite suddenly at the age of twenty, she announced that she was ready to be confirmed. Her mother wrote to the rector, Mr. Burgess:

Last, though not least, I ask you in gladness of heart, if you can call to-morrow afternoon, between four and five, and see my dear Mary, on subjects of immortal interest, to which that her attention is in any degree turned, I give thanks to God. . . .[357]

Ten days later she was confirmed.

Andrew proved a more difficult case. When he was young Mrs. Sigourney comforted herself with an article by Chauncey A. Goodrich called ''Hints on the Conversion of Children,'' which said that

parents should not expect their children ordinarily to be exercised with as deep, or as protracted distress, as persons of maturer age. . . . They have not sinned as flagrantly or as long . . . Although guilty, their stains are by no means of so crimson a die. . . .[358]

Mary had at least been conscious that it was not quite respectable to remain unconverted; but Andrew as he grew older did not seem to feel the slightest shame for his position. He began to talk of going west, where one could shake off the trammels of society, where a man was judged by his real character instead of his church affilia-

tion. His mother had inherited from Mr. Huntley some
land in Indiana, part of a grant to Revolutionary soldiers; he would settle on it and grow up with the country.
Wealth and happiness might be found there on the banks
of the Wabash; at all events one would not be constantly
cross-examined about the state of his soul.

Mrs. Sigourney prayed each day that Andrew's heart
might be softened; and those friends who were in her
confidence she asked to set apart a certain time on Sunday when, wherever they were, they would join in her
supplication. She soon wrote to Mrs. Whittlesey, who
edited the *Mother's Magazine* in New York, suggesting a
concerted prayer by all Christian mothers for the conversion of their children.

I thank you too for the appointment you have made with me
for Sabbath morning [Mrs. Whittlesey replied]. Nothing could
have been more grateful to my feelings.—I had for some time
previous thought of making a similar request of my dear
brothers & sisters. We have all of us children who have hitherto
refused to cast in their lot with the people of God.
How little children reflect into what depths of distress they
may plunge their anxious parents by neglecting to give their
hearts to the Saviour, in youth, and in health. . . .
Since the receipt of your letter I have written many letters
. . . extending the invitation to Christian Mothers & without
once giving your name I have said that the proposal was first
made by a mother for her *only son*. . . .
I have thought it might be well for parents to engage their
Pastors to pray every Sabbath for *unconverted children*—and
for *young men*.[359]

The only effect of the good ladies' supplication seemed
to be to increase Andrew's uncommunicative habits. A
heavy dejection settled upon him; whole days would pass

with scarcely a word beyond the ordinary greetings to members of the family. As winter set in, the solitary walks grew shorter and were succeeded by long periods during which he shut himself up in his room, coming out only for meals, at which he sat silent and ate little. Mrs. Sigourney wrote one of his friends about this time:

The remainder of us are well, unless it may be Andrew, who, I think pines after you, and has established a still more austere system of seclusion. The rule of the monks of La Trappe, might be better borne by him, than by most young men of nineteen. . . .[360]

Soon, however, his depression betrayed a physical source: the indisposition he had called cold and influenza proved to be consumption. His strength ebbed swiftly away, and with it some of the reticence that had so troubled his mother. When all the other members of the family had retired, she would sit for hours, stroking the long hair back from his forehead, while, eyes flashing with an unnatural luster, he would unfold elaborate plans for his new life in the West.[361] On the subject of religion, however, he was evasive as ever, and her pious heart was fain to content itself with the thought that the Father's ear needs not the "vain pomp of speech."

Rather ashamed that his mother supported herself by writing, Andrew had always been steadfast in refusing all gifts from her, except at Christmas and birthdays. But as the disease progressed, he gradually lost this pride, and began to delight in the little attentions that were showered upon him. His meticulous habits suffered no change, and until the last he was about the house, collecting his effects, filing correspondence, and destroying papers. Several years before he had been very much annoyed when his mother published some of his school exercises—little essays on Temperance and Studies—without his knowledge;[362] and resolving that his "Thought Books" should not appear likewise, he burned them himself, except for one or two of the earlier volumes, which his mother had intentionally mislaid.

One day in June when the odor of the hop blossoms filled the house, he complained that the bright sun hurt his eyes. His mother soon covered the windows with heavy, opaque curtains.

Then he said calmly, and in a clear voice,—"I am dying.—I cannot see you." Bending over him [Mrs. Sigourney wrote], I heard the only admission of pain that he had uttered. A suppressed intonation,—scarcely above a sigh,—breathed the single word, *"sharp!"* It was never repeated. The death pangs, however keen, were borne in silence.

Fixing on his watch, a look of intense inquiry, he took it from its place by his bedside, wound it with a perfectly steady hand, and said,—"At twelve o'clock, I shall be gone." . . .

Kneeling beside him, the last trembling prayer was poured forth, in which we were ever to join on earth. After that, he spoke not. Physician, clergymen, and neighbors, who had been hastily summoned, surrounded him, but he spoke not. He was no longer in communication with those we call the living.

Gently, and gradually, respiration continued to shorten, but there was no resistance, no moaning. As the clock struck the hour of high noon, and the hand of his own watch touched the point of twelve,—he fell asleep, like an infant on the breast of its mother. . . .[363]

The next day an English artist was employed to take a portrait of him in the coffin. The features bear such a resemblance to those of Mrs. Sigourney that one would think the painter sketched from her, as she hovered over her son. The kindly brush eliminated all marks of disease except for a slight prominence of the cheek bone that is not unbecoming. But the mother was disappointed: ''The outline of the brow, and contour of the features, are correct,—but the expression of sadness is too deep, and the eye defective both in color and irradiation,'' she wrote.[364]

In 1850 obituaries were regarded as the only proper conclusion to a good life. Their composition was usually attributed to a desire to console the sorrowing friends or to a pious wish that the unfailingly noble example of the deceased might inspire virtue in others. But the real reason for the popularity of these ''memorial volumes'' lies deep in the current of sentimentality that ran through the nineteenth century. Young gentlemen, bereaved of their sweethearts, pressed locks of hair in their Bibles and haunted graveyards. But the truly sentimental lovers, while they avoided friends to give themselves unreservedly to grief, found most exquisite pleasure in sharing their sorrows with the whole world. Feelings too personal to discuss at home they published as poems. Assured of a ''gallery,'' they followed Rousseau along the lake, joyfully weeping. ''Combien de fois,'' says he, ''m'arrêtant pour pleurer à mon aise, assis sur une grosse pierre, je me suis amusé à voir tomber mes larmes dans l'eau!''[365] In the forties and fifties much of American literature was busy with the contemplation of its tears, with ''melting,'' and ''la plus douce mélancholie.'' The general spirit is admirably expressed by what one little girl said of the *Death of an Infant:* ''It makes me sad, but not unhappy.''[366]

Mrs. Sigourney had written half a dozen obituary volumes since 1816, when she published the tribute to Nancy Hyde, her associate in the Norwich school. She was soon at work on *The Faded Hope,* an account of Andrew,

Andrew M. Sigourney

Engraved from a Painting by Hunt Taken after Death.

which appeared two years after his death. The preface
was short:

It was thought by friends, who had seen the childish writings
of the subject of this sketch, that a selection of them might be
interesting and suggestive to those of similar age. In making
such selections, and connecting them by links of a brief life,
but little varied by incident, a sorrowing heart has found solace, and has been aided more fervently to say, "The Lord gave,
and the Lord hath taken away: blessed be the name of the
Lord."

The "childish writings" are extracts from the volumes
of Andrew's journal that Mrs. Sigourney had tucked
away during his illness. Those influential "friends" who
"induced" and "persuaded" her to publish at least half
her works would certainly have urged selections from the
rest of the diary if it had been saved. But her chief interest in *The Faded Hope* was neither Andrew's diary
nor his life: it was his death. "Physician, clergymen, and
neighbors" had been summoned to watch the spectacle;
now the whole world was invited to look on. A fifth of the
264-page volume is devoted to his illness—the "resistless
cough," the "perilous night-sweats," the "hectic fever,"
the "increasing emaciation," the "cold damps on the
forehead," and other less pleasant matters: "Tumefac-
tion of the feet had been visible for a few days, and his
flesh wasted like a snowwreath."[367] To us the book seems
in deplorable taste, the more so that a mother wrote and
sold it. But Mrs. Sigourney should not be too harshly
blamed for printing such stuff; had not the great Irving
himself put his name to a worse sketch of the Misses
Davidson? She was simply following the fashion.

How had the fashion arisen? The Greeks had been
more interested in living than in dying. "I to my death,

you to live on," said Socrates; "but which of these is
best, God alone knows."[368] Among English writers there
are some like Shakespeare and Burton who shared the
skeptic's uncertainty of the nature of death. Others,
more orthodox, like Milton or George Herbert, looked beyond it to the future glory the Bible promised. They
found

> death like sleep,
> A gentle wafting to immortal life.[369]

But the figure most often applied was *mors janua vitae,*
death the gate of life. In the eighteenth century, largely
through the popularity of Young's *Night Thoughts,* this
conception came to prevail. Gay infidels like Lorenzo and
Lysander were solemnly warned that

> The knell, the shroud, the mattock, and the grave;
> The deep, damp vault, the darkness, and the worm[370]

still held all their terrors for those who rejected salvation. "Instead of sumptuous Tables, and delicious
Treats," declare Hervey's *Meditations,* "the poor Volup-
tuary is Himself a Feast for fattened Insects; the Reptile
riots in his Flesh."[371] But to a true believer death was the
"rescuer," the "crown of life," "victory"; and the
"gloomy pass" soon becomes the "soft transition." The
deathbed, quite naturally, offers the supreme test of a
man's religion; no hypocritical conformer can deceive
this "detector of the heart." Here of all places

> You see the man, you see his hold on Heaven.[372]

It was to witness this preliminary judgment that the
friends and neighbors gathered at the dying Christian's
bedside.

His God sustains him in his final hour!
His final hour brings glory to his God!
Man's glory Heaven vouchsafes to call her own.
We gaze, we weep; mix'd tears of grief and joy!
Amazement strikes: devotion bursts to flame:
Christians adore! and infidels believe![373]

The "graveyardism" of the nineteenth century derived directly from the school of *Night Thoughts.* The
"beautiful death" became a tradition of the Practical
Ideal. It was the climax of life. Every respectable person died nobly with appropriate last words, which sometimes, as in the case of John Quincy Adams, had to be
written by the witnesses themselves.[374] Little children,
roused from sleep, were brought to watch a sick brother
set out on the great journey much as if he were going
away to school; and for weeks after their dreams were
filled with vivid images gathered from illustrated Bibles
and the conversation of their elders. One fourteen-year-
old girl dreamed of her lately deceased brother Theron.
He was

standing on an eminence, and beyond him in the blue sky, she
saw a gate, which presently opened, and little Frank [who
died at the age of three] accompanied by a female attendant of
angelic form . . . came thro' it. He was dressed in a robe of
white bespangled with gold. In his hand he carried a harp,
upon which he played, while another, tastefully adorned, was
suspended on his left arm.

And while she watches, Theron, aged one year and eight
months, is dressed in the robe, given the harp, and led
into the city.[375]

About 1830, however, people began to feel less certain
that the scriptural account of the next world could be ac-

cepted literally. They lingered with more anxious scrutiny on this side of the dark threshold, while their attention shifted from the spiritual glories beyond to the physical phenomena accompanying the transition. They brooded over the abnormalities of the deathbed, celebrating them in copious verse. The normal old man of three-score and ten, dying calmly in his bed, is rarely a subject for the "graveyard" poet, whose dying hero is almost invariably young. If the wicked met an untimely end, so, to be sure, did the virtuous, the Faded Hopes, who declined and died before they had reached their teens.

Some of this preoccupation with early death can be ascribed to physical causes. The dead children, for example, who pass in such pathetic array through nineteenth-century literature unquestionably reflect the fearful infant mortality that took away about half of them before they were five years old.[376] Tuberculosis, causing fully half the deaths of adolescents,[377] explains much about the pale maidens who languish and die so meekly in Victorian novels. Today with infant mortality at about 7 per cent and tuberculosis enormously reduced, the Paul Dombeys and Little Nells have no successors in our literature.

Before the cause was properly understood, diseases were regarded by the pious as visitations of God to which the virtuous would submit without repining. The Practical Ideal went farther, and even made them useful. Sickness, says *The Father's Book*, is one of the chief means of improving the heart. When it arrives the well-informed parent is

prepared to say: "I thank thee that disease has been so long delayed. . . . Make this illness useful to me and my family. . . . Give me penitent feelings and holy joys; and while I have this opportunity, in thy mercy afforded me, to reflect on Thee and myself, and to display my character to my children, may my mind be guided, and my conduct controlled agreeably to thy will, for the benefit of us all." . . .

If he shrinks with horror from the approach of death, if he sees only gloom before him,—he who has brought them to the belief that the Gospel affords a deliverance from its terrors, how can they ever regard it as the golden gateway to a happier life?[378]

The people who read this in 1834 were probably not aware of any insincerity in Dwight's counsel. Their faith had withstood the attacks of Tom Paine and the Deists at the beginning of the century; but, while gentlemen did not discuss them, the crude old arguments were still at work beneath the surface. And now the so-called Higher Criticism was making it more and more difficult to accept the literal infallibility of the Bible, an assumption upon which Protestant society had rested since the Reformation. Faith itself seemed to totter if one admitted that Moses had not written the Pentateuch nor Isaiah every word of the prophecy that bears his name. And like uncertain children who grow more vehement in maintaining a doubtful statement, the poets reiterated louder and louder their belief in the traditional conception of a future life. "There is no death!" they cried.

> It is not death to fling
>   Aside this sinful dust,
> And rise on strong, exulting wing,
>   To live among the just.[379]

Good and bad alike floated to the skies on the flowery beds of ease so scorned by Isaac Watts,[380] while their friends set to work on obituary poems with the eager refrain, "There is no death!"

There were plenty of strong souls in the Victorian age whose ''piping took a troubled sound''[381] when they chose to struggle with their doubts rather than drown them out with the cymbals of conformity. It was not as

> Light half-believers of our casual creeds[382]

that Clough and Arnold awaited the spark from heaven. Tennyson, faltering and falling

> Upon the great world's altar-stairs,

still stretched ''lame hands of faith'' and groped for light.[383] And in 1855, three years after *The Faded Hope* was published, Walt Whitman burst into the darkened funeral chamber, sounding

> triumphal drums for the dead.
> I fling through my embouchures the loudest and gayest music to them.[384]

''You forget you are sick,'' he says *To One Shortly to Die;*

> you do not mind the weeping friends, I am with you,
> I exclude others from you, there is nothing to be commiserated,
> I do not commiserate, I congratulate you.

To him the Grim Reaper is ''lovely and soothing death,'' the ''dark mother,'' the ''strong deliveress,'' whom he greets with glad carols and dances under the high-spread sky, joyously singing the dead. To him too the future is a mystery, but he does not fear it.

DAREST thou now O soul,
Walk out with me toward the unknown region,
Where neither ground is for the feet nor any path to follow?

No map there, nor guide,
Nor voice sounding, nor touch of human hand,
Nor face with blooming flesh, nor lips, nor eyes, are in that land.

I know it not O soul,
Nor dost thou, all is a blank before us,
All waits undream'd of in that region, that inaccessible land.

Till when the ties loosen,
All but the ties eternal, Time and Space,
Nor darkness, gravitation, sense, nor any bounds bounding us.

Then we burst forth, we float,
In Time and Space O soul, prepared for them,
Equal, equipt at last (O joy! O fruit of all!) them to fulfil O
soul.[385]

Mrs. Sigourney could never have felt at home in such
a heaven; it was the very antithesis of hers. She had
often pictured the scene: she would hear familiar voices
first; then as her dazzled eyes grew accustomed to the
splendor, she would make out the faces of her loved ones
—her "sainted father," Madam Lathrop, her mother, old
Mr. Wadsworth; and before them all there would be a
grave, young face, whose violet eyes no longer hid dark
thoughts in their troubled depths. Such a faith as hers,
firmly established fifty years before when she knelt at
Madam Lathrop's bedside, was impervious to the Higher
Criticism; and Andrew's death, far from weakening it,
had given greater strength through the exercise of resignation. Mr. Dwight's son had been taken too at the age of
nineteen; here was an added bond of sympathy between
them. Did he ever find it hard to see a blessing in the
loss? She wrote June 11, 1853:

. . . God has been leading us in some measure with the same
wise discipline, "under the cloud, and through the sea." His

Name be praised! Why should it not be so, and with the same
strain, as when he suffered us to stand in the broad sun-light,
and twine the flexile tendrils of hope around earthly props,
with that hidden exulting love, that turned the heart from
Him?

Sometimes, I feel as if it was arrogant for us to mourn, as if
we had a right to claim anything as our own, we, who stand
upon the earth & breathe the air, but as mendicants, liable
without a moment's warning to be ejected from our frail ten-
ure, and be remembered no more. Far more fitting is it for us,
to busy ourselves about the service that God appoints, than to
question and wonder at his ways. I am sure that such thoughts
have often passed through your own mind, and that you have
not only felt that it was good for you to be afflicted, but that
you would not be willing, for your soul's sake to have passed on
without these afflictions. I well know how the return of this
most beautiful season will bring back to your heart, and that of
the Mother, countless mournful recollections of the fair sleeper,
over whose pillow the turf gathers greenness. Every rose, every
strawberry, seems encircled by *his* pale hand that rejoiced in
their first blush, and ripeness. "Even so, Father, for so it
seemed good in Thy sight."[386]

Submission was no mere pose with Mrs. Sigourney.
Her whole life she had busied herself about the service
God appointed without questioning his ways. One by one
the earthly props had been taken from her: her marriage
proved disappointing; the financial worry that beset her
girlhood had returned to shatter the dream of a prosperity that would permit abounding charity; and when
she turned her affection to Andrew, that hope too had
faded. Yet with serene faith in God she could still say,
"Even so, Father."

On the last day of December, 1854, she was so busy
signing and wrapping books for New Year's gifts that

she hardly heard Mr. Sigourney come home and go to his room. When the supper hour arrived, he did not appear. Suddenly alarmed, she hurried upstairs and found him dead of apoplexy. He was seventy-six years old.

Three sentences in her autobiography announce his death:

. . . No previous confinement had precluded his attention to his professional business. Morning and noon of his last day on earth found him as usual at his store, from whence he walked home, but at the setting of the sun entered on that glorious life which hath no end.[387]

Is it perhaps significant that among her thousands of elegiac poems there is none to his memory?

CHAPTER SEVEN

PAST MERIDIAN

T HE first months of widowhood were spent caring
for her stepson, Charles Sigourney, a middle-aged
bachelor, who died of consumption in June, 1855.
The character of their relations during the thirty-five
years since she had dressed him in "mazarine-blue bombazine" is purely conjectural, for she makes no further
mention of him. His decease brought forth no obituary
volume nor poetical lament; and in her autobiography
Mrs. Sigourney, ordinarily exact in such statistics, records his death as occurring two and a half years after
Mr. Sigourney's, though it was really only six months.[388]
In October, Mary, the last jewel in "the maternal
heart's rifled casket,"[389] was married to the Rev. Francis T. Russell, and went to live in New Britain, where her
husband was rector of St. Mark's church. Her departure
left Mrs. Sigourney quite alone and free from the necessity of consulting anyone's convenience but her own.
With serene optimism she settled down to grow old gracefully. From the beginning of her career she had laid
aside a part of the profits from her work and invested it
shrewdly; and with the small estate Mr. Sigourney left,
she was in comfortable circumstances. But dearer to her
than wealth was the homage she enjoyed as the most fa-

mous person in Hartford. From the bishop down everyone attended her parties in honor of visiting celebrities.
Held up as their model, her manners were the despair of
schoolgirls. The prim little figure in black satin was already a tradition in the minds of the younger generation.
One little girl who really wrote very well was so over-
awed by the great lady's inquiry about her "chirography" that she deprecated her skill and received a lecture
she was never to forget on careless writing as "a minor
immorality."[390]

The town hoodlums, however, were not so easily terri-
fied by Mrs. Sigourney's fame. When her apples were
ripe they came over the fence

in the evening with baskets and barrows, and, discovering there
was no man upon the premises, waxed bolder and bolder. The
accustomed phrases of dismission and dispersion failed to put
them to flight. Rappings at the window, and commands to dis-
appear, they met with a dogged defiance. I grieve to say that,
in impudence of deportment, the girls were conspicuous. Since
the usual forms of objurgation were powerless, I bethought me
of another expedient. I said pleasantly: "Come in at the gate,
to my south piazza, and I will give you apples." There I kept
a large reservoir [a barrel?], and put some into every dirty
hand, assuring them that all who would not help themselves
should be thus supplied. They seemed content, and eventually
their faces brightened at being called the children who would
not take what did not belong to them. . . . So a rude species of
mission-school sprang out of this apple traffic.[391]

In former days respect for age came without bribes, she
thought; and her eyes filled with tears as she turned
toward the corner of the room—the sacred corner—
where her blessed father's staff still stood beside the
cushioned chair he brought with him from Norwich.[392]

Her house was crowded with such relics, many of which seemed ugly or commonplace to callers unaware of the sentiments that surrounded them. There were tall carved cabinets, filled with souvenirs of other days. On the little square piano stood vases of flowers, both artificial and real, with bits of china, glass, and silver bric-a-brac, the "clutter" of those days. The *papier-mâché*-covered desk still displayed the little writing box from Lady Blessington; and the brass-mounted, claw-legged table, laden with gifts from the great, held also a model of Mrs. Sigourney's own hand in marble, incredibly white and slender against the dark velvet.[393] But even surrounded by memories, her days were often lonesome.

I was troubled at meeting you a day or two since [she wrote a young friend], because I fancied you were looking thin, and not quite well. If this is so, I hope you will take great care of yourself on my account as well as that of others; for I have not as many friends to love as I once had, and I shall always love you for your kindness to my poor boy, over whose fair, young head, rest the clods of the valley.[394]

A young lady invited to tea one evening was ushered into this museum of a drawing-room. Soon Mrs. Sigourney appeared, a short little body with "soft, patrician" hands shown off to good advantage against the full, black satin dress. The flaxen curls, not yet quite gray, were carefully arranged under the fine lace cap, from which floated wide satin ribbons. She greeted her guest with a little curtsy, and led the way into the dining-room. After a silent blessing, the maid, Ann Prince—Black Ann—who had lived with the family for twenty-five years, came out of the shadows to place a silver tureen on the table. Mrs. Sigourney served the creamed oysters, her heavy rings flashing in the candlelight, while one caught occa-

Lydia H. Sigourney

From a Daguerreotype. By Permission of The Connecticut
Historical Society.

sional glimpses beneath the lace sleeve of the bracelet, now quite commonly ascribed to Queen Victoria. Next came another dish, more massive, of solid silver, which, being uncovered, disclosed a delicious plate of "baked beans, golden brown, and sending forth a most appetizing aroma." Mrs. Sigourney smiled as she served them, saying: "My dear young friend, I have always preserved the good old-fashioned custom of having baked beans Saturday night, and I hope you will enjoy them as much as I do." The whole meal, from oysters to caraway cookies and quince sauce, combined simple fare with the elaborate service of an earlier day.[395]

Year by year her books appeared, fat volumes, for the most part, of three to four hundred pages. But of the fourteen published after 1850 only four or five can be said to be new work. *Past Meridian* (1854), a treatise on old age, filled with illustrations from history and biography, ancient and modern, contains her best and simplest prose. A romantic poem about Aaron Burr's conspiracy with Blennerhassett in an Ohio swarming with parrakeets gave its name to *The Western Home,* published the same year. *Lucy Howard's Journal* (1857) was a narrative in diary form of the education of a young girl early in the century. *The Daily Counsellor* (1859), a collection of Bible texts for each day in the year, followed by an original poem suggested by it, proved the most popular of her later books; and this like most of the other works was a compilation from earlier writings. *Letters to My Pupils* (1851) included a generous reprinting from the perennial sketch of Nancy Hyde, as well as a 125-page section entitled *My Dead,* composed of tributes and biographies of her former pupils. *Olive Leaves* (1851) gathered up all the poetry and prose she had written on the subject of peace. *Sayings of the Little Ones and Poems for Their Mothers* (1854) describes itself. So do the two volumes of pious biographies called *Examples of Life and Death* (1851) and *Examples from the Eighteenth and Nineteenth Centuries* (1857), each containing about 350 pages. And in *The Man of Uz* (1862) a metrical version of the book of Job stands at the head of 276 pages of elegies, principally of Hartford worthies, unrelieved by any other sort of poem.

The reputation so firmly established in the forties lived on into the next decade,[396] though fewer of her books were reprinted, and accounts with her publishers sometimes showed a deficit that pointed to Mrs. Sigourney as her own best customer. Her formulas remained unchanged. Other "female poets," sweet songsters with whom the woods were vocal, had learned the trick, while thoughtful readers found Mrs. Sigourney's work less interesting than that of Mrs. Browning and George Eliot. The undercurrent of honest disparagement, which had never been entirely lacking, was held in check through respect for the woman rather than her poetry. Some rebuffs there were, to be sure. Her native city of Norwich had steadfastly refused to accept her as its laureate. For the anniversary of the Academy she wrote by request a lyric which the chief musician scornfully declined to sing, and it was read among the prose exercises.[397] Some of the poems she wrote for the bicentennial of the founding of the town were likewise omitted from the memorial volume, which found space for works of far less merit.[398] There was solace in the appreciation of Hartford, however, that more than compensated for these ungracious slights: in 1862 a new thoroughfare opened across Farmington Avenue was named Sigourney Street in her honor.[399]

As the fountains of poesy ran low, her acts of philanthropy increased. In 1811 when the Norwich school was opened, she had marked out in an old-fashioned account book the plan of devoting one-tenth of all her income to charity, a plan from which she never deviated unless to enlarge her donations.[400] The Indians, the Greeks, missionaries in Asia and Africa as well as at home, regularly received her unobtrusive gifts. The poor and the sick in Hartford were constantly being supplied with clothes and provisions. While she entertained callers or meditated verses, her knitting needles were never idle; her systematic record shows that in 1860 alone she made eleven pairs of stockings in addition to sixty-nine other garments.[401] A physician of extensive practice remarked that he found Mrs. Sigourney's baskets for the sick "in every direction."[402] She remembered the anniversaries of old people when their own children forgot. Frequent visits and gifts showed her interest in the work of charitable institutions. To several of them, including the Reform School at Meriden, she regularly sent barrels of apples from her orchard and cakes at Easter time; and one of her benefactions was a sum of money for the purchase of hens, which the boys were to care for, receiving in return the profit from the sale of eggs to the institutions.[403] The Orphan Asylum, the Deaf and Dumb Asylum, the State Prison, the Retreat for the Insane were all objects of her benevolence. Individual cases, too, she relieved with earnest care. Utter strangers appealed to her for help in getting work as governesses or teachers; and many grateful letters bear witness to her generous response. A man sent to prison for stealing some of her jewelry was so touched by her attention to his "spiritual and temporal wants" that after his release, it is said, he called to tell her "that her kindness had changed his character, and that henceforth he hoped to be an honest man and a good Christian."[404]

Abolition, the greatest humanitarian movement of the century, had surprisingly little effect on Mrs. Sigourney's poetry. Although she had none of the fervor of Whittier or Mrs. Stowe, she did not lack interest in the question. As a child in Norwich she had known several former slaves; and one of her first efforts at teaching was a free school held twice a week for poor children, one class of which was composed entirely of negroes,[405] at a time, too, when they were not commonly admitted to the schools.[406] She had helped from the beginning with the work of the Colonization Society; and her early attitude toward slavery is shown in a poem called "The First Slave Ship," sent to its *African Magazine* in 1825:

> First of that race which curst the wave,
>   And from his rifled cabin bore,
> Inheritor of woe,—*the slave*
>   To bless his palm-tree's shade no more, . . .
>
> Know'st thou within thy dark domain
>   The horrors of thy prison'd freight?
> The fetter'd chieftain's burning tear,
>   The parted lover's mute despair,
> The childless mother's pang severe,
>   The orphan's agony are there. . . .
>
> Oh Africk! what has been thy crime?
>   That thus like Eden's fratricide,
> A mark is set upon thy clime,
>   And every brother shuns thy side?[407]

An even closer acquaintance with the race began when Ann Prince came to work for her. Great as her affection was for this faithful creature, shrewd common sense told Mrs. Sigourney that immediate enfranchisement of the negroes was neither wise nor practicable. And when the clouds of war began to gather, her advice to the slave was not that of the Abolitionist,

> To shake aloft his vengeful brand
> And rend his chain apart,[408]

but rather to wait in humility for the future life,

> Look to the mansions of the free!
> .   .   .   .   .   .
> Look to that realm where chains unbind,—
> Where the pale tyrant drops his rod,
> And where the patient sufferers find
> A friend,—a father in their God.[409]

From a letter she wrote to Gen. Sam Houston on February 11, 1861,[410] it seems clear that she did not contemplate a war to maintain the Union:

Since I last wrote, the dark signs of the times have become more manifest, and portentious. We can no longer shut our eyes upon them.

And must we indeed, make shipwreck of the happiest Government that the world has seen? Will we soon, abandon an experiment that foreign nations watched with admiration and envy?

Well, if this result must come, simple Philosophy, as well as the dictates of religion, move us to meet it, in the best way we are able. But I pray you, my dear General Houston, if within the scope of possibility, to save Texas, if it may not be to the whole Union, at least to what shall be our division of it. Is not the northern portion favorably disposed towards us? . . .

I speak not as a politician, but as a friend, *confidentially.* Keep my wishes safe and sacred in your heart, and if you are not able to keep the "whole herd from rushing violently down a steep place into the sea," still hold back Texas, and bind it to us in the golden chain of brotherhood.

Two months later the cannon were roaring at Sumter and the struggle was on. Day by day the wounded were brought home; each issue of the *Courant* carried fresh news of casualties and military funerals. Such events, fitting so easily into the old formulas, had always provided material for verses. But Mrs. Sigourney was apathetic, her heart was not stirred. As her life drew to a close the conviction that war of any kind was wrong grew stronger within her; and the only writings inspired by the four years of strife were a few poems for the newspapers. Elegies came from her pen with unceasing regularity, but they were for the old friends—Mr. Colt, and Mr. Tudor, and even Mr. Beach, who had supplanted her husband in the bank.

As the end of the war approached, Mrs. Sigourney had completed her autobiography, *Letters of Life* (parts of which had appeared in *Letters to My Pupils* in 1851), and had begun work on a last long poem that was to be called *The Septuagenarian.* It was never finished. In March, 1865, two weeks before Lincoln's assassination, she became ill, and on the tenth of June she died. The house was filled with the odor of the vine blossoms as it had been fifteen years before when the Faded Hope left her. And that evening at sunset the bells of the city, which she had heard on her first visit sixty years before, were tolled for an hour, while people from all walks of life thronged the house for a last look at their friend.

She had outlived her generation. Her poems were "classics" in the sense that everyone talked of them, but few read them; and the writer of the long obituary notice in the *Courant* betrayed his unfamiliarity with her works when he commended them for simplicity.

Her merit, in our judgment, greatly consists in the rigid restraint with which she curbed in herself, the national tendency to redundancy and inflation of style, giving us in her writings, prose as well as verse, models of pure and elegant English. . . . Had she indulged in that rhetorical tumescence and bombast, which is so easy, and yet so commonly admired, she would have scattered far and wide the seeds of a false taste, and a meretricious style, which would not have been easily or soon eradicated. On the contrary, she contributed to educate the national taste, and instruct the literary judgment of our people, by the purity and simplicity of her rhetoric, as much as she has elevated and ennobled their sentiments by the deeply religious tone, which pervades all her writings.[411]

Tributes even more glowing were paid to her memory; but none of them could long preserve her literary reputation. Even the "Christian Benevolent Lady"[412] seemed in danger of being forgotten. A fund of nearly $1,000 was subscribed to erect a statue or suitable memorial at her grave in Spring Grove Cemetery; but the large subscriptions heading the list and representing some of the first families of Hartford remained unpaid. The committee finally collected $220, which included a gift of $5.00 from the Orphan Asylum in Auburn, New York, and the present monument was put in place.

In 1887 a tablet was installed in Christ Church. There is an old story, impossible now to verify, that an argument among the vestrymen about the position of the organ was responsible for some of the zeal that was shown

for this memorial. But Mr. Whittier, who supplied the
verse, well remembered the kindness Mrs. Sigourney
showed him during his youth in Hartford, and there can
be no doubt of his sincerity.

> She sang alone, ere womanhood had known
> The gift of song which fills the air to-day.
> Tender and sweet, a music all her own
> May fitly linger where she knelt to pray.

BIBLIOGRAPHY

The following list includes all the works of Mrs. Sigourney that were published as books under her supervision. No effort has been made to collect her contributions to periodicals, which would number many thousands; and, similarly, single poems reprinted for distribution at funerals or for other occasions have been excluded. Where the same work reappeared under a new title, the second title is listed with a reference to the earlier one. The dates in all cases are taken from the title-pages, though many of the books were published late in the preceding years to catch the holiday trade. I have been unable to examine the four books marked with an asterisk.

Moral Pieces, in Prose and Verse. By Lydia Huntley. (Hartford, 1815.)

The Writings of Nancy Maria Hyde, of Norwich, Conn. Connected with a Sketch of Her Life (Norwich, 1816). [Anonymous.]

The Square Table (Hartford, 1819).
    [An anonymous pamphlet; two numbers were issued: No. I. Hartford: published by Samuel G. Goodrich, September 1, 1819. P. B. Gleason & Co., Printers. Price 12½ cents. No. II. *The Square Table, or Meditations of Four Secluded Maidens Seated around It* (Hartford, November 1819).]

Traits of the Aborigines of America. A Poem (Cambridge, 1822). [Anonymous.]

Sketch of Connecticut Forty Years Since (Hartford, 1824). [Anonymous.]

Poems; by the Author of "Moral Pieces in Prose and Verse." (Boston and Hartford, 1827.)

*Female Biography (Philadelphia, 1829). [Anonymous.]

*Biography of Pious Persons (Springfield, 1832). 2 volumes. [Anonymous.]

Evening Readings in History (Springfield, 1833). [Anonymous.]

The Farmer and Soldier. A Tale (Hartford, 1833). [Signed L. H. S. Reprinted in *Olive Buds,* 1836.]

How To Be Happy. Written for the Children of Some Dear Friends. By a Lady. (Hartford, 1833.)

The Intemperate [by Mrs. Sigourney], *and the Reformed* [by Gerrit Smith] (Boston, 1833).
[Reprinted in *Sketches,* 1834.]

Letters to Young Ladies. By a Lady. (Hartford, 1833.)

Memoir of Phebe P. Hammond, a Pupil in the American Asylum at Hartford. Prepared for the Press by Mrs. L. H. S. (New York, 1833.)

Report of the Hartford Female Beneficent Society (Hartford, 1833). [Anonymous.]

Poems (Philadelphia, 1834).
[Beginning with the third edition, 1838, this book was known as *Select Poems.* The contents were slightly changed from time to time.]

Poetry for Children. By the Author of *How To Be Happy.* (Hartford, 1834.)

Sketches (Philadelphia, 1834).

Tales and Essays for Children (Hartford, 1835).

Memoir of Margaret and Henrietta Flower (Boston, 1835). [Anonymous.]

Zinzendorff, and Other Poems (New York and Boston, 1835).

History of Marcus Aurelius, Emperor of Rome (Hartford, 1836).

Olive Buds (Hartford, 1836).

Poems for Children (Hartford, 1836).
[An abridgment of *Poetry for Children,* 1834.]

*History of the Condition of Women (Boston, 1837).

The Girl's Reading-book . . . (New York, 1838).

Letters to Mothers (Hartford, 1838).

The Boy's Reading-book . . . (New York, 1839).

The Religious Souvenir for 1839 (New York, 1839). [Edited.]

Memoir of Mrs. Mary Ann Hooker (1840).

The Religious Souvenir for 1840 (New York, 1840).
[Edited.]

Pocahontas, and Other Poems (London, 1841).
[Published in London before Mrs. Sigourney's departure, and in New York a few weeks later.]

Poems, Religious and Elegiac (London, 1841).

Letters to Young Ladies. New Edition with Two Additional Letters. . . . (London, 1841.)

Pleasant Memories of Pleasant Lands (Boston, 1842).

Poems (Philadelphia, 1842).
[Published by John Locken. The plates were later acquired by Leavitt & Allen and used for many years.]

The Pictorial Reader . . . (New York, 1844).
[This title was claimed by another, and that of *The Child's Book* . . . was substituted.]

The Lovely Sisters (Hartford, 1845).
[A revised edition of the *Memoir of Margaret and Henrietta Flower*, 1835.]

Poetry for Seamen (Boston, 1845).
[The whole edition of 1,000 copies was bought by Martin Brimmer for distribution by a sailors' chaplain.]

Scenes in My Native Land (Boston, 1845).

Myrtis; with Other Etchings and Sketchings (New York [copyright, 1846]).

The Voice of Flowers. (Hartford, 1846).

The Weeping Willow (Hartford, 1847).

Water-drops (New York, 1848).

The Young Ladies' Offering; or Gems of Prose and Poetry. By Mrs. Sigourney; Mrs. Hemans; Mrs. Howitt; Eliza Cook; Miss Barrett; Miss Landon; and others. (Boston, 1848.)
[Edited.]

Illustrated Poems . . . (Philadelphia, 1849).

Poems for the Sea (Hartford, 1850).
[Reprints most of *Poetry for Seamen*, 1845, with some additional pieces and illustrations by William Lawrence.]

Whisper to a Bride (Hartford, 1850).

Letters to My Pupils: with Narrative and Biographical Sketches (New York, 1851).

Examples of Life and Death (New York, 1852).

Margaret and Henrietta (New York [copyright, 1852]).
[A reprint of *The Lovely Sisters*, 1845.]

Olive Leaves (New York, 1852).

Voices of Home; or Poems for the Sea (Hartford, 1852).
[A reprint of *Poems for the Sea*, 1850, except that the first poem is placed in a different position.]

The Faded Hope (New York, 1853).

Memoir of Mrs. Harriet Newell Cook (New York, 1853).

Past Meridian (New York and Boston, 1854).

The Western Home, and Other Poems (Philadelphia, 1854).

Sayings of the Little Ones, and Poems for Their Mothers (Buffalo and New York, 1855).

Examples from the Eighteenth and Nineteenth Centuries. First Series. (New York, 1857.)

Lucy Howard's Journal (New York, 1858).

The Daily Counsellor (Hartford, 1859).

Gleanings (Hartford and New York, 1860).

The Man of Uz, and Other Poems (Hartford, 1862).

Selections from Various Sources (Worcester, 1863).

Sayings of Little Ones (New York, 1864).
[A reprint of the first three parts of *Sayings of the Little Ones, etc.*, 1855.]

The Transplanted Daisy. Memoir of Frances Racilla Hackley (New York). [Privately printed. Anonymous.]

Letters of Life (New York, 1866). [Posthumous.]

NOTES

CHS = Connecticut Historical Society, Hartford.
NYPL = New York Public Library.
NYHS = New York Historical Society.

1. Sigourney, *Letters of Life* (New York, 1866), p. 75.
2. *Ibid.*, pp. 13–18.
3. *Record of Connecticut Men in . . . the Revolution*, ed. Henry P. Johnston (Hartford, 1889).
4. Mrs. S. always wrote her mother's name *Sophia; Zerviah* is the form that appears in genealogical records.
5. See *Life and Letters of Catharine M. Sedgwick*, ed. Mary E. Dewey (New York, 1871), p. 26.
6. *Letters of Life*, p. 110.
7. *Ibid.*, pp. 110–111.
8. *Ibid.*, p. 57.
9. *Ibid.*, p. 56.
10. Sigourney, *Sketch of Connecticut Forty Years Since* (Hartford, 1824), p. 22. Many details for this chapter have been drawn from pp. 1–30.
11. *Letters of Life*, p. 42.
12. Mrs. S. to Theodore Dwight (1796–1866), July 25, 1845. NYPL.
13. Hannah F. Gould to Mrs. S., January 8, 1844. CHS.
14. *Letters of Life*, p. 76.
15. *Ibid.*, p. 78.
16. *Ibid.*, p. 79.
17. *Ibid.*, p. 83.
18. *Ibid.*, p. 84.
19. Now in the Watkinson Library, Hartford. It was really presented two years later, August 12, 1807.
20. Lydia Huntley, *Moral Pieces, in Prose and Verse* (Hartford, 1815), p. 19.
21. The school opened May 13, 1811. See [Sigourney], *The Writings of Nancy Maria Hyde . . .* (Norwich, 1816), p. 137.
22. *Letters of Life*, p. 197.
23. *Ibid.*, p. 191.

24. Alma Lutz, *Emma Willard: Daughter of Democracy* (Boston and New York, 1929), p. 52. Quotations from this book are by permission of, and special arrangement with, Houghton, Mifflin Company.

25. *Letters of Life*, p. 216.

26. *Ibid.*, p. 217.

27. *Ibid.*, p. 236.

28. August 1, 1833. Trinity College, Hartford.

29. Daniel Wadsworth to Lydia Huntly [*sic*], August 27, 1814. Trinity.

30. *Ibid.*, November 9, 1814. CHS.

31. *North American Review*, I (May, 1815), 111.

32. *Letters of Life*, p. 240.

33. *Ibid.*, p. 243.

34. *Ibid.*, p. 71.

35. *Ibid.*, p. 243.

36. *Hours at Home*, I (October, 1865), 560.

37. Quotations in this paragraph are from *Letters of Life*, pp. 243–244.

38. *Ibid.*, p. 251.

39. *Ibid.*, pp. 252–253.

40. *Ibid.*, p. 245.

41. *Ibid.*, p. 246.

42. *Ibid.*, p. 253.

43. *Ibid.*, p. 255.

44. *Ibid.*, p. 260.

45. *Ibid.*, p. 262.

46. *Ibid.*, p. 84. I have changed *is* to *was*.

47. *Ibid.*, p. 264.

48. Francis Parsons, *The Friendly Club and Other Portraits* (Hartford, 1922), p. 171.

49. *Letters of Life*, p. 267. Jane Carter married Mr. S. May 25, 1803, and died January 24, 1818.

50. [Sigourney], *Traits of the Aborigines of America* (Cambridge, 1822), p. 74.

51. *Ibid.*, p. 76.

52. *Ibid.*, pp. 77–78.

53. *Ibid.*, p. 123.

54. *Ibid.*, pp. 120–121.

55. *Ibid.*, p. 160.

56. *Ibid.*, p. 167.

57. *Ibid.*, pp. 169–170.

58. *Ibid.*, p. 98.

Notes 181

59. Meshshahmeyah, a Choctaw, to Mrs. S., April 17, 1824. CHS.

60. David Folsom, a Choctaw, to Mrs. S., June 17, 1824. CHS.

61. *Connecticut Courant*, September 7, 1824.

62. [Sigourney], *Poems; by the Author of "Moral Pieces in Prose and Verse"* (Boston and Hartford, 1827), pp. 84–85.

63. See the journal kept by Mrs. S., May 9–30, 1825. CHS, uncatalogued.

64. Sereno Edwards Dwight, *The Greek Revolution, An Address, Delivered in Park Street Church, in Boston, . . . April 1, 1824,* p. 27.

65. *Poems* (1827), p. 13.

66. See Mrs. S. to Theodore Dwight, November 2 and 15, 1830, and Mrs. S.'s MS copy of the orations. NYPL.

67. See Stamatiades' letters to Mrs. S., 1838–1845, CHS.

68. William Williams, "O'er the Gloomy Hills of Darkness." See *The New Laudes Domini*, ed. Charles S. Robinson (copyright, Century Co., 1892), No. 1129.

69. Arthur Cleveland Coxe, in Robinson, *op. cit.*, No. 1121.

70. Reginald Heber, "From Greenland's Icy Mountains," in Robinson, *op. cit.*, No. 1119.

71. Sigourney, *Poems* (Philadelphia, 1842), p. 74.

72. *Letters of Life*, p. 275.

73. *Poems* (1827), pp. 69–71. On p. 70 the name appears *Thorlasken;* the proper spelling is *Thorlaksson*.

74. Mrs. S. to Dwight, November 2, 1830. NYPL.

75. *Ibid.*, January 14, 1832. NYPL.

76. *Ibid.*, May 7, 1832. NYPL.

77. *Letters of Life*, p. 259.

78. Mrs. S. to Dwight, January 14, 1832. NYPL.

79. *Ibid.*, May 3, 1833. NYPL.

80. *Ibid.*, October 27, 1834. NYPL.

81. Eliza Leslie to Mrs. S., December 12, 1839. CHS.

82. Meade Minnigerode, *The Fabulous Forties* (New York and London, 1924), p. 131.

83. Louis A. Godey to Mrs. S., September 14, 1839. CHS.

84. Mrs. S. to Thomas W. White, June 14, 1834. NYHS.

85. Mrs. S. to Messrs. Lea & Blanchard, July 25, 1839. NYPL.

86. Sigourney, *The Weeping Willow* (Hartford, 1847), pp. [v]–vi.

87. *Ibid.*, p. vi. Gray's *Elegy* reads "*rustic* moralist," st. 21.

88. J. Orville Taylor to Mrs. S., August 12, 1839. CHS.

89. See William B. Sprague to Mrs. S., July 17, 1839. CHS; and

Mrs. S. to William C. Little, August 5, 1839. Historical Society of Pennsylvania.

90. December 2, 1836. CHS.

91. January 24, 1837 (dated 1836, but changed by Mrs. S.). CHS.

92. December 30, 1836. CHS.

93. Mrs. S. to Miss Lynch, December 27, 1836. NYHS.

94. Charles Sigourney, *To the Stockholders of the Phœnix Bank, Hartford, Conn.* [June 26, 1837.]

95. George Beach, *To the Stockholders of the Phoenix Bank.* [August 8, 1837.]

96. Charles Sigourney, *To the Stockholders of the Phœnix Bank, Hartford, Conn.* [August 25, 1837], p. 10.

97. ''Farewell to a Rural Residence,'' in Sigourney, *Pocahontas, and Other Poems* (New York, 1841), p. 94.

98. Dr. Jonas King to Mrs. S., July 24, 1838. CHS.

99. ''Maternal Efforts'' in *The Mother's Magazine,* VI (1838), 5.

100. *Letters of Life,* p. 275.

101. Almira Hart Lincoln Phelps to Mrs. S., October 16, 1838. CHS.

102. Emma Willard to Mrs. S., August 23, 1839. CHS.

103. *Ibid.,* September 28, 1841. CHS.

104. Sigourney, *Whisper to a Bride* (Hartford, 1850), p. 45.

105. *Ibid.,* p. 57.

106. Mrs. S. to Dwight, May 24, 1832. NYPL.

107. Sigourney, *The Faded Hope* (New York, 1853), p. 45.

108. Ithiel Town to Mrs. S., January 21, 1839. CHS.

109. Theodore Dwight to Mrs. S., September 20 and November 7, 1839. CHS.

110. *Letters of Life,* p. 373.

111. *Ibid.,* p. 340.

112. The CHS has Mrs. S.'s record for 1860–61; it was reproduced in *The New England Magazine,* XXVII (1902), 25.

113. *Letters of Life,* p. 367.

114. *Ibid.,* p. 376.

115. J. N. Danforth in *The Family Circle,* ed. H. A. Graves (Boston, copyright, 1843), p. 15.

116. John Angell James: selections in *The Wedding Gift, or the Duties and Pleasures of Domestic Life* (Boston, copyright, 1843).

117. *The Marriage Ring: or How To Make Home Happy* (Boston, copyright, 1843), p. 34.

118. Graves, *op. cit.,* p. 10.

119. Quoted from Vinet in *Gems for the Bridal Ring*, ed. Jeremiah E. Rankin (Boston, 1868), p. 103.

120. Milton, *Paradise Lost*, iv, 635–638.

121. Rankin, *op. cit.*, p. 92.

122. Cf. Arthur W. Calhoun, *Social History of the American Family* (3 vols.; Cleveland, 1917), II, 88.

123. *The Wedding Gift*, p. 95.

124. *Woman's Rights Tracts* (1851), No. 5.

125. Eliza Southgate to Moses Porter, quoted in Calhoun, *op. cit.*, II, 134.

126. *Pocahontas*, pp. [132]–133.

127. *Poems* (1842), p. 109.

128. *Pocahontas*, pp. [194]–195.

129. *Ibid.*, p. 190.

130. Sigourney, *Pleasant Memories of Pleasant Lands* (Boston, 1842), p. 4.

131. *Ibid.*, p. 213.

132. *Ibid.*, p. 273.

133. Nathaniel S. Wheaton, *Journal of a Residence during Several Months in London . . . in the Years 1823 and 1824* (Hartford, 1830), p. 149.

134. Lutz, *Emma Willard*, pp. 138–139.

135. *Pleasant Memories*, p. 274.

136. R. Shelton Mackenzie to Mrs. S., March 6, 1838. CHS.

137. *Pleasant Memories*, pp. 48–49.

138. John Frazer to Mrs. S., July 6, 1840. CHS.

139. J. A. Froude, *Letters and Memorials of Jane Welsh Carlyle* (3 vols.; London, 1883), I, 128.

140. *Ibid.*, I, 275.

141. *Ibid.*, I, 67.

142. This letter, here first published, is in the collection of Mr. James Hillhouse of New Haven.

143. *Jane Welsh Carlyle: Letters to Her Family, 1839–1863*, ed. Leonard Huxley (New York, 1924), pp. 77–78. By permission of Doubleday, Doran Co.

144. *Pleasant Memories*, pp. 245 ff.

145. John Dowling to Mrs. S., February 5, 1846. CHS. Final title was *Burial of Mrs. Judson*.

146. *Pleasant Memories*, p. 249.

147. *Ibid.*, p. 274.

148. *Ibid.*, p. 249.

149. *Ibid.*, p. 262.

150. *Ibid.*, pp. 257–261.

151. P. 68.

152. See Mrs. Fry's letter to Mrs. S., March 13, 1841. CHS.

153. Mrs. S. to the Rev. [George] Burgess, February 3, 1841. NYHS.

154. *Faded Hope,* p. 157.

155. Mrs. Jameson to Mrs. S., n.d. CHS.

156. *Pleasant Memories,* pp. 353–354.

157. *Ibid.,* p. 356.

158. Maria Edgeworth to Mrs. S., March 4, 1842. CHS.

159. *Ibid.*

160. Alexander H. Everett to Mrs. S., May 15, 1842. CHS.

161. March 18 [1841]. CHS.

162. Joanna Baillie to Mrs. S., August 20, 1841. CHS.

163. CHS.

164. Mrs. S. to Lady Blessington, June 10, 1841. Quoted from R. R. Madden, *The Literary Life and Correspondence of the Countess of Blessington* (3 vols.; London, 1855), II, 314–315.

165. *Ibid.,* II, 316. May 28, 1842.

166. Lady Blessington to Mrs. S., September 30, 1842. CHS.

167. Mrs. S. to Lady B. In Madden, *op. cit.,* II, 318. October 31, 1842.

168. *Pleasant Memories,* p. 51.

169. *Ibid.,* pp. 53–55.

170. *London Athenaeum,* April 15, 1843, p. 369.

171. *Brother Jonathan,* May 20, 1843, p. 77.

172. See Mrs. Hall's letter to Mrs. S., August 24, 1843, CHS, and *The London Britannica* for April, 1843.

173. Mrs. S. to Professor Silliman, July 14, 1843. Boston Public Library.

174. *London Athenaeum,* May 20, 1843, p. 488.

175. *Pleasant Memories,* pp. 282–283.

176. Mary Russell Mitford to Mrs. S., n.d. CHS.

177. Maria Edgeworth to Mrs. S., September 4, 1843. CHS.

178. *Ibid.,* May 14, 1844. CHS.

179. *Ibid.,* February 24, 1846. CHS.

180. See *Select Poems,* 10th ed., 1850.

181. H. A. Beers, *Nathaniel Parker Willis* (Boston, 1899), pp. 80–81.

182. E. A. Poe, *Complete Works,* ed. James A. Harrison (17 vols.; New York, 1902), XVI, 117. By permission of the Thomas Y. Crowell Company.

183. Beers, *op. cit.,* p. 67.

184. J. F. Cooper, *Correspondence of James Fenimore-Cooper* (2 vols.; New Haven, 1922), I, 227.

185. The earliest use of this title I have noted is *Blackwood's*, XXXV (May, 1834), 807; but it was certainly in use earlier.

186. *Poetical Works of Mrs. Felicia Hemans* (5th Am. ed.; 2 vols.; New Haven: Nathan Whiting, 1828), II, 172–173.

187. Poe, *op. cit.*, XVI, 7.

188. *Ibid.*, XVI, 12.

189. *Ibid.*, VIII, xiv.

190. *Ibid.*, XVII, 33–35.

191. *Ibid.*, XVII, 37–38.

192. Sigourney, *Poems* (Philadelphia, 1834), pp. [13]–16.

193. *Ibid.*, pp. 190–193.

194. Sigourney, *Gleanings* (Hartford and New York, 1860), p. 126–128.

195. *Pocahontas*, p. 14.

196. *Ibid.*, p. 26.

197. *Gleanings*, p. 96.

198. *Pleasant Memories*, p. 351.

199. Sigourney, *Poetry for Seamen* (Boston, 1845), p. 13.

200. *Ibid.*, p. 19.

201. *Poems* (1842), p. 113.

202. *Ibid.*, p. 114.

203. *Ibid.*, p. 115.

204. *Poems* (1834), p. 168.

205. *Ibid.*, p. 69.

206. *Ibid.*, p. 23.

207. *Faded Hope*, p. 221.

208. Sigourney, *The Western Home, and Other Poems* (Philadelphia, 1854), p. 20.

209. *Letters of Life*, p. 262.

210. Sigourney, *Zinzendorff, and Other Poems* (New York and Boston, 1835), p. 2.

211. O. W. Holmes, *Poetical Works* (Boston, 1891), I, 17–18.

212. Mrs. S. to Dwight, August 20, 1855. NYPL.

213. *Letters of Life*, p. 74.

214. *Ibid.*, p. 36.

215. *Ibid.*, p. 107.

216. *Pocahontas*, sts. liii and lv, pp. 31–32.

217. *Irish Quarterly Review*, V (June, 1855), 193 ff.

218. Reprinted in *Illustrated Poems* from *Pleasant Memories*, pp. 57–62.

219. *Poems* (1834), p. 138.

220. Quoted by Beers in *The Memorial History of Hartford County*, ed. J. H. Trumbull (Boston, 1886), I, 163.

221. A. H. Everett in *Democratic Review*, N. S. XI (Sept. 1842), 247.

222. J. R. Lowell, *Writings* (10 vols.; Boston, 1892), III, 308.

223. Rev. Samuel F. Jarvis to Mrs. S., April 12, 1832. CHS.

224. H. Teagle to Mrs. S., January 4, 1836. CHS.

225. Lowell, *op. cit.*, II, 153.

226. Thomas B. Read, *The Female Poets of America* (6th ed.; Philadelphia, 1855), pp. 187–191.

227. *National Portrait Gallery* (Philadelphia: Longacre, 1839), IV, 6.

228. *North American Review*, XLI, 442.

229. *Ibid.*, p. 445.

230. *Ibid.*, p. 442.

231. Poe, *op. cit.*, XVI, 12.

232. From a pamphlet biography by Ann Stephens. (NYPL *C p.v.743 No. 7, p. 265.)

233. Ezekiel Bacon, *Vacant Hours* (Utica, 1845).

234. Mrs. S. to Judge Ezekiel Bacon, November 13, 1845. Berkshire Athenaeum and Museum, Pittsfield, Mass.

235. *America of the Fifties: Letters of Fredrika Bremer*, ed. Adolph B. Benson (New York, 1924), pp. 39–40.

236. Mrs. S. to the Rev. Robert Waterston, May 6, 1847. NYHS.

237. *Ibid.*

238. *Letters of Elizabeth Barrett Browning*, ed. F. G. Kenyon (1897). Mrs. B. to H. S. Boyd, April 3, 1845, p. 251.

239. A good example is found in Miss Huntley's letter to Mr. and Mrs. Enoch Noyes, September 3, 1818, owned by Mrs. Elford Trowbridge of New Haven.

240. *Letters of Life*, p. 374.

241. *Ibid.*, p. 373.

242. William H. Prescott to Mrs. S., January 8, 1845. CHS.

243. *Poems* (1834), p. 79.

244. *American Monthly Magazine*, IV, 275.

245. Mrs. S. to Lady Blessington, June 10, 1841. In Madden, *op. cit.*, II, 314.

246. August 12, 1843. *Ibid.*, II, 315–316.

247. Louis A. Godey to Mrs. S., September 14, 1839. CHS.

248. Lutz, *Emma Willard*, p. 189.

249. *Godey's Lady's Book*, May, 1841.

250. *Ibid.*, June, 1841.

251. *Ibid.*, July, 1841.

252. *Ibid.*, September, 1841.

253. Emma Willard to Mrs. S., August 23, 1839, September 28, 1841, and September 18, 1846. CHS.

254. W. M. Griswold, *Passages from the Correspondence and Other Papers of Rufus W. Griswold* (Cambridge, 1898), p. 102.

255. *Ibid.*

256. CHS.

257. R. W. Griswold, *Poets and Poetry of America* (Philadelphia, 1842), p. 538.

258. CHS.

259. See Mrs. Hale's reply, March 22, 1842. CHS.

260. Emma Willard to Mrs. S., September 18, 1846. CHS.

261. *Ladies' Companion*, May, 1843.

262. *Ibid.*, June, 1842.

263. Emma C. Embury to Mrs. S., March 24, 1843. CHS.

264. *Ibid.*, April 18, 1843. CHS.

265. *Ladies' Companion*, XVII (September, 1842), 283; XVIII (November, 1842), 52.

266. *Ibid.*, January, 1844.

267. Ann Stephens to Mrs. S., December 19, 1843. CHS.

268. *The New World*, VII (December 30, 1843), 779.

269. This letter and the one following have never before been published. CHS.

270. *Graham's Lady's and Gentleman's Magazine*, XX (January, 1842), No. 1, p. 72.

271. R. W. Griswold, *Poets and Poetry of America*, p. 190.

272. Ann Stephens to Mrs. S., April 27, 1843. CHS.

273. See letters of the Hon. J. D. Doty to Mrs. S., March 7, 1839, April 16, 1840, and December 20, 1846. CHS.

274. Alexander H. Everett to Mrs. S., October 25, 1839. CHS.

275. *Pocahontas*, p. 16.

276. *Ibid.*, p. 17.

277. *Ibid.*, p. 19.

278. *Ibid.*, p. 20.

279. *Ibid.*, p. 23.

280. *Ibid.*, p. 24.

281. *Ibid.*, p. 25.

282. *Ibid.*, p. 28.

283. *Ibid.*, p. 29.

284. *Ibid.*, p. 30.

285. R. W. Griswold, *Female Poets of America* (1849), p. 91.

286. Mrs. S. to Messrs. Key & Biddle, July 15, 1834. Historical Society of Pennsylvania.

287. Mrs. S. to Munroe & Co., June 15, 1844. Yale.

288. *Ibid.*, January 19, 1845. Yale.

289. Martin Brimmer. See *Letters of Life*, p. 351.

290. In 1854 *Letters to Mothers* reached the sixth edition and *Letters to Young Ladies* the sixteenth. The tenth edition of *Select Poems* (1834) appeared in 1850.

291. *Letters of Life*, p. 355.

292. By George Freeman. See his letter to Mrs. S., September 19, 1842. CHS.

293. Mrs. S. to Carey & Hart, April 14, 1848. NYHS.

294. *Ibid.*, April 20, 1848. NYHS.

295. *Ibid.*, June 28, 1848. NYHS.

296. *Ibid.*, August 22, 1848. NYHS.

297. *Ibid.*

298. *Illustrated Poems.*

299. Samuel Rogers to Mrs. S., October 25, 1848. CHS.

300. Sigourney, *Past Meridian* (New York and Boston, 1854), p. 19.

301. New York, 1897, pp. 341–342.

302. Mrs. S. to Carey & Hart, January 10, 1848. NYHS.

303. Joel Hawes, *Lectures to Young Men* . . . (Hartford, 1829), p. 84.

304. *Ibid.*, p. 112.

305. *Ibid.*, p. 56; *prospered* seems meant for *prosperous.*

306. *Ibid.*, p. 58.

307. [Jacob Abbott], *Cousin Lucy's Conversations* (Auburn, New York, 1850), p. 63.

308. William A. Alcott, *The Boy's Guide to Usefulness* (Boston, 1846), p. [9].

309. *Ibid.*, pp. 13–14.

310. *Ibid.*, pp. 14–15.

311. *Ibid.*, p. 25.

312. *Ibid.*, p. 36.

313. *Ibid.*, pp. 40–41.

314. *Ibid.*, p. 38.

315. *Ibid.*, p. 55.

316. *Ibid.*, p. 50.

317. *Ibid.*, p. 51.

318. *Ibid.*, p. 75.

319. *Ibid.*, p. 77.

320. *Ibid.*, p. 80.

321. *Ibid.*, p. 89.

322. Theodore Dwight, Jr., *The Father's Book* . . . (Springfield, 1835), pp. 162–163.

323. Alcott, *op. cit.*, p. 112.

324. A. P. Stanley, *Life and Correspondence of Thomas Arnold, D.D.* (London, 1844), II, 159.

325. Alcott, *op. cit.*, p. 113.

326. Hawes, *op. cit.*, p. 129.

327. Dwight, *op. cit.*, p. 61. '' (I call three years an advanced age in this case,).''

328. *Ibid.*, pp. 151–152.

329. *Ibid.*, p. 80.

330. *Ibid.*, pp. 82–83.

331. *Ibid.*, p. 84.

332. Hawes, *op. cit.*, p. 37.

333. *The Publications of the American Tract Society*, Series V, vol. 1, p. [104.

334. *Ibid.*, pp. [122– [124.

335. *Letters of Life*, p. 49.

336. *Faded Hope*, p. 97.

337. *Ibid.*, p. 88.

338. *Ibid.*, p. 134.

339. *Ibid.*, p. 106.

340. *Ibid.*, p. 135.

341. *Ibid.*, p. 131.

342. *Ibid.*, p. 64.

343. *Ibid.*, p. 96.

344. *Ibid.*, p. 47.

345. *Ibid.*, pp. 63–64.

346. *Ibid.*, p. 109.

347. *Ibid.*, p. 74.

348. *Ibid.*, p. 155.

349. *Ibid.*, p. 129.

350. *Ibid.*, pp. 188–191.

351. Trinity College.

352. Sigourney, *Olive Leaves* (New York, 1852), p. 48.

353. *Ibid.*, p. 33.

354. *Faded Hope*, p. 183.

355. Dolly P. Madison to Mrs. S., March 22, 1849. CHS.

356. *Faded Hope*, pp. 194–195.

357. Mrs. S. to the Rev. [George] Burgess, May 20, 1847. NYHS.

358. *Mother's Magazine*, VI (1838), 82.

359. Mrs. A. G. Whittlesey to Mrs. S., January 28, 1848. CHS.

360. Mrs. S. to Mr. Worth, January 11, 1850. NYHS.

361. *Faded Hope*, p. 215.

362. *Ibid.*, pp. 166, 173.

363. *Ibid.*, pp. 235–236.

364. *Ibid.*, p. 236.

365. J.–J. Rousseau, *Les confessions* (2 vols.; Paris: Flammarion, n.d.), I, 154.

366. R. Shelton Mackenzie to Mrs. S., May 30, 1837. CHS.

367. *Faded Hope,* p. 232.

368. Plato, *Apol. Socratis.* Quoted by Burton, *Anatomy of Melancholy* (New York, 1924), p. 408.

369. Milton, *Paradise Lost,* xii, 434.

370. Edward Young, *Night Thoughts* (Boston, 1842), iv, 10–11.

371. James Hervey, *Meditations and Contemplations* (15th ed.; London, 1760), I, 76.

372. *Night Thoughts,* ii, 643.

373. *Ibid.,* ii, 677–682.

374. See *New York Times,* October 10, 1926, IX, 11: 7.

375. Mrs. F. L. A. Gookins to Mrs. S., November 19, 1846. CHS.

376. The earliest reliable statistics are found in John S. Parry, ''Infant Mortality, etc.,'' in *Papers of the Social Science Association of Philadelphia,* 1871.

377. See Karl Pearson, *The Fight against Tuberculosis and the Death-rate from Phthisis* (London, 1911). Cf. George A. Evans, *Handbook of Historical and Geographical Phthisiology,* 1888.

378. Dwight, *Father's Book,* pp. 63–64.

379. G. W. Bethune, ''It Is Not Death to Die'' in *New Laudes Domini,* ed. Charles S. Robinson, No. 1156.

380. Isaac Watts. ''Am I a Soldier of the Cross?'' Robinson, *op. cit.,* No. 749, st. 2.

381. Matthew Arnold, *Thyrsis.*

382. *Ibid., The Scholar Gypsy.*

383. Tennyson, *In Memoriam,* lv.

384. Walt Whitman, *Leaves of Grass,* 1855, ''Song of Myself,'' st. 18.

385. Quoted from *The Chief American Poets,* ed. C. H. Page (Boston, etc. [1905]), p. 595.

386. NYPL.

387. *Letters of Life,* p. 321.

388. The records of Christ Church Parish show that Mr. S. was buried December 30, 1854, *æ.* 76, and Charles H. S., June 30, 1855, *æ.* 46. Cf. *Letters of Life,* p. 321.

389. Mrs. S. to Samuel Rogers, March 17, 1852. In P. W. Clayden, *Rogers and his Contemporaries* (1889), II, 426.

390. *Hartford Times,* December 3, 1915.

391. *Letters of Life,* pp. 392–393.

392. *Ibid.,* p. 393.

393. Louise J. R. Chapman, ''A Visit to Mrs. Sigourney,'' *Connecticut Quarterly,* I, 47–49.

394. Mrs. S. to Elizabeth Sheldon, May 29, 1852. CHS, uncatalogued.

395. Details in this paragraph from Chapman, *op. cit.*

396. The decline of Mrs. S.'s reputation was rapid. In 1892 Beers (*Initial Studies in American Letters*, p. 175) refers to her as ''a Hartford poetess, formerly known as 'the Hemans of America,' but now quite obsolete.'' Kipling, however, lists her among the authors in the Headmaster's study in ''The Last Term'' (*The Complete Stalky & Co.* [London, 1929], p. 390): ''there were hundreds of volumes of verse—Crashaw; Dryden; Alexander Smith; L. E. L.; Lydia Sigourney; Fletcher and a purple island; Donne; Marlowe's *Faust*. . . .''

397. *Letters of Life*, p. 380.

398. John W. Stedman, *The Norwich Jubilee* (Norwich, 1859). The hymn of welcome is printed, however, on p. 47.

399. Albert L. Washburn and Henry R. Buck, *History of Hartford Streets* (Municipal Art Society of Hartford, 1911), p. 73.

400. *Letters of Life*, p. 410.

401. Grace Lathrop Collin, ''Lydia Huntley Sigourney,'' *New England Magazine*, XXVII, 25.

402. *Hours at Home*, I (October, 1865), 563.

403. Mrs. S. to Dr. Hatch, September 10, 1861. Owned by Mrs. Russell G. Andrews.

404. *Hours at Home*, I (October, 1865), 563.

405. *Letters of Life*, p. 200.

406. James Truslow Adams, *History of New England* (3 vols.; Boston, 1927), III, 367.

407. Mrs. S. to the Rev. Randolph Gurley, October 28, 1825. NYHS. Printed with slight variations in *Poems* (1827), p. 176.

408. J. G. Whittier, ''To William Lloyd Garrison,'' in *Complete Poetical Works*, Cambridge ed. [copyright, 1894], p. 262.

409. *Poems* (1827), p. 177.

410. In the Archives of the Texas State Library. Copy supplied by Mr. Garland Greever.

411. *Hartford Courant*, June 12, 1865.

412. Mrs. S. is so called in the subscription list for her memorial. CHS, uncatalogued.

INDEX

Stamatiades, Demetrius, 31–32, 40, 69

Stephens, Ann, 72, 99, 115, 116, 117, 119

Sterne, Laurence, 4

Stewart, C. S., 40

Story Teller, The, 71

Stowe, Harriet Beecher, 40, 170

Sultan of Turkey, 32

Sumter, Fort, 172

Swift, General, 29

Talfourd, Thomas Noon, 119, 120

Tennyson, Alfred, 160

Thackeray, W. M., 95

To a Dying Infant, 95

To a Land Bird at Sea, 120

To the Cactus Speciosissimus, 95

Tommy Wellwood, 143–144

To-morrow, 93–94

Tower of London, 56

Town, Ithiel, 44

Tracy, Dr. Philemon, 6

Traits of American Life, 108

Traits of the Aborigines, 23–26, 84, 125

Tricoussi, orations of, 32

Trinity College, Hartford, 21, 30, 147

Tucker, N. Beverley, 119

Tuckerman, Henry T., 114

Tudor, Samuel, 172

Tuileries, The, 54, 60, 61

Tussaud's, Madame, 56

Uncle Tom's Cabin, 23

Victoria, Queen, 63, 72, 167

Village Blacksmith, The, 107

Virginia, 29, 33, 84

Voice of Flowers, The, 130

Wadsworth, Daniel, 7, 8, 9, 11–14, 17, 21, 24, 27–29, 40, 72, 131, 161

Wadsworth, Mrs. Daniel, 7

Wadsworth, Eunice, 8, 17

Wadsworth, Jeremiah, 6, 7

Wadsworth, Mrs. Jeremiah, 6, 7, 9

Wakefield's *Botany,* 18

Washington, George, 6, 28, 29, 60, 148

Washington College, see Trinity College

Water-Drops, 130

Watts, Isaac, 159

Wayland, Francis, 65

Webster, Daniel, 133–134

Wedgwoods, The, 58

Weeping Willow, The, 130

Welby, Mrs., 120

Welsh, Helen, 57

Wentworth, Zerviah, see Huntley, Mrs. Ezekiel

West Hoboken Institute, 39

West Point, 148–149

Western Home, The, 167

Westminster Abbey, 56

Whisper to a Bride, 43–44

Whitman, Walt, 160

Whittier, John G., 15, 170, 174

Whittlesey, Mrs. A. G., 151

Willard, Emma, 9, 10, 43, 54, 108, 110, 113

Williams, John, 40, 51

	DATE DUE		